100 DINOSAURS FROM A TO Z

By Ron Wilson

Illustrated by Cecilia Fitzsimons

Prepared with the cooperation of Dr. Paul C. Sereno,
Department of Vertebrate Paleontology,
American Museum of Natural History.

Publishers • GROSSET & DUNLAP • New York
A member of The Putnam Publishing Group

Copyright © 1986 by Patrick Hawkey & Company, Ltd.
All rights reserved. First published in the United States in
1986 by Grosset & Dunlap, a member of The Putnam
Publishing Group, New York.
Printed in Great Britain. Library of Congress
Catalog Card Number: 86-80774 ISBN 0-448-18992-5
A B C D E F G H I J

Contents

Acanthopholis

Acanthopholis was an ankylosaur—or "armored dinosaur". The group of dinosaurs to which Acanthopholis belonged are called nodosaurids. These creatures carried their heavy bodies on short legs. Their armor gave them good protection, with bony plates covering exposed body parts.

Spines projected from the sides of the dinosaur's body, but its underside had no protection and could have been easily damaged when the dinosaur was attacked by theropods. Unlike some of the other ankylosaurs, Acanthopholis did not have a club at the end of the tail.

These armor-plated lizards had very weak jaws with small teeth. Their diet probably consisted of plants and some soft flesh, perhaps from small insects. The teeth would have been able to deal with this.

In time of danger Acanthopholis, like the other ankylosaurs, would probably have crouched close to the ground. This would have been possible because of the short legs.

A study of the head showed that its length was greater than its width, and that there were spikes protruding from the neck.

Weight 2 US tons (1.8 tonnes)
Length 18 feet (5.5 meters)
Found southern England
Lived Late Cretaceous

Acanthopholis

Acrocanthosaurus

Acrocanthosaurus was a member of a group of dinosaurs known as spinosaurids. These dinosaurs were very large animals and had spines sticking out from their backs. From a study of the skeletons, these spines were found to be extensions of the vertebrae – the bones which make up the backbone.

It is thought that, unlike some of the other spinosaurids, Acrocanthosaurus did not have a large skin sail (see Spinosaurus or Altispinax). However, it may have had a skin sail attached to its spines, which would probably have helped

Acrocanthosaurus

the dinosaur to control its body heat. When more is known about the creature, it may turn out to be a special megalosaurid and not a spinosaurid.

The name Acrocanthosaurus means "very spiny lizard," a reference to the spines which jutted out from the dinosaur's backbone. The spines were about 12 inches (30 centimeters) in length, and there may have been a thick layer of muscle under the skin through which they grew.

Acrocanthosaurus was a large dinosaur and a vicious carnivore, catching and killing other animals for food.

Weight not known
Length 40 feet (12 meters)
Found Oklahoma, USA
Lived Early Cretaceous

Alamosaurus

Alamosaurus belonged to a large group of dinosaurs which were known as sauropods. The word sauropod means "lizard feet" and these creatures have rightly been dubbed "dinosaur giants." Their feet had five toes like the lizards which still roam the earth today.

These large creatures were plant-eaters and they inhabited areas where there was plenty of plant life. Early theories about sauropods suggested that they lived in the water because only water could support such large bodies. Water would also have given the creatures protection

Alamosaurus

from their enemies. But this idea has been challenged as more and more new information is collected.

Alamosaurus has been named after Alamo, the fort where the famous siege took place. This dinosaur belonged to the group known as the titanosaurids, or "giant lizards." This is not a very good description since many of the titanosaurids were quite small. In many cases only small pieces of skeletons have been found.

Weight 30 US tons (27 tonnes)
Length 67 – 69 feet (20 – 21 meters)
Found Texas, Utah, New Mexico, and
  Montana, USA
Lived Late Cretaceous

Albertosaurus

Albertosaurus was named after Alberta in Canada where one skeleton was found. This dinosaur belonged to the group of tyrannosaurids, or "terrible lizards." The best known of these is Tyrannosaurus rex.

Although smaller than this ferocious beast, Albertosaurus was still a very dangerous creature. When hungry, it attacked and killed other animals living nearby. With its great size and strength it must have had little resistance from smaller animals. Scientists are not sure what Albertosaurus caught, killed, and ate. It may be that the creature's large size prevented it from moving quickly. This would have made it impossible for it to catch faster animals. If this were so, it would probably have had to scavenge for at least some of its food. However, Albertosaurus may have been able to capture and kill some of the dinosaurs which had very thick armor plating.

Inside the enormous head of the Albertosaurus were such ferocious teeth that they would make short work of any animal, tearing the flesh apart quickly and easily.

There was a complete contrast between the hind legs, which were thickly built, and the front ones, which were thin and less powerful. The creature would have walked on its hind legs.

Weight 2 US tons (1.8 tonnes)
Length 26 feet (8 meters)
Found Alberta, Canada; Montana, USA
Lived Late Cretaceous

Albertosaurus

Allosaurus

Allosaurus was as long as a bus. It had giant jaws, with razor-sharp, pointed teeth. Ferocious claws grew from each of three fingers on the hands. The skull was large but made of thin bones, with thicker areas where protection was needed. In spite of the skull size, Allosaurus had only a small brain.

Weight 1 – 2 US tons (1 – 2 tonnes)
Length 42 feet (12.8 meters)
Found North America, Africa, Australia, and possibly Asia
Lived Late Jurassic

Altispinax

Altispinax was a spinosaurid, with long spines which stuck out from its back. These were outgrowths from the vertebrae – the small bones which make up the backbone. An examination of these projections showed that they were four times as long as the bones which they were growing from.

It is likely that these outgrowths were covered with skin which formed a sail. Scientists think that this sail was useful in two ways. The male spinosaurid may have used his raised sail as a warning to other males. It was probably no more than a threat, because if he had engaged in fighting his sail would have been damaged.

The sail may also have been useful as a "radiator." When turned to the sun it trapped heat which warmed the dinosaur's body. When turned away from the sun it caused heat to be lost from the dinosaur's body, and so it would cool down.

Altispinax means "high thorn," so named because of the projections.

Weight not known
Length 26 feet (8 meters)
Found northwest Europe
Lived Early Cretaceous

Allosaurus

Altispinax

Anchiceratops

Anchisaurus

Anchiceratops

Anchiceratops – "near horned face" – belonged to the group of creatures known as ceratopsians. These were horned dinosaurs which evolved on the Earth late in the Age of Reptiles. Perhaps it was because of this that they throve and were found in large numbers. They were among the larger creatures of the dinosaur world.

A unique feature of the ceratopsians was the neck frill, which was different on each dinosaur. By its neck frill the creature could be recognized by others of its kind. It probably used its horns and other protrusions for defending itself against the attacks of meat-eaters.

Skeletons have been found in Canada, where the creature lived by browsing on tough vegetation.

Weight not known
Length 19 feet 6 inches (6 meters)
Found Alberta, Canada
Lived Late Cretaceous

Anchisaurus

Anchisaurus means "near lizard" or "close reptile," and it belonged to the anchisaurids. With its bladelike teeth Anchisaurus fed on plants. Its strong thumb claws could have been used for holding on to its food.

Weight 60 pounds (27 kilograms)
Length 7 feet (2.2 meters)
Found South Africa; Connecticut, USA
Lived Late Triassic/Early Jurassic

9

Ankylosaurus

Ankylosaurus

The ankylosaurs were armored lizards which varied greatly in size. The largest was as long as a bus, while the smallest was not much bigger than a man.

Ankylosaurs were extremely sturdily built with armor plates, knobs, and spikes which were embedded in the leathery skin. These plates went from the head to the tail but did not cover the sides of the body.

Ankylosaurus – the "fused lizard" – was the largest of the ankylosaurs, but in spite of its size and frightening appearance it fed only on plants. With its small teeth and weak jaws the dinosaur could take only plants which could be easily bitten off. At the end of the head, which was covered with armor plates, was a horny beak which did not have any teeth.

Flesh-eating carnosaurs were potentially dangerous to the ankylosaurs. As an added means of self-defense the ankylosaur had a club on its tail. The creature may have been able to swing the club with great force and aim a savage blow at an enemy.

Weight 3 – 4 US tons (1.8 – 2.7 tonnes)
Length 35 feet (10.7 meters)
Found Montana, USA; Alberta, Canada
Lived Late Cretaceous

Antarctosaurus

Antarctosaurus was one of the group of sauropods, or "lizard feet." The creatures probably fed on plants which they stripped off using their teeth. With such long necks they could reach up high to pick at the best vegetation which many other creatures were unable to reach.

Antarctosaurus probably had a gizzard into which the plants passed. Here there were stones which the animals had swallowed and which helped to grind up the plant material. Constant action by the stones inside the gizzard made them round and smooth. Large numbers of these stones have been found. Another idea is that the plant material went into the stomach where bacteria helped to break it down so that it could be used.

It was once thought that the sauropods went into the water to avoid their enemies. This now seems unlikely as their enemies would have followed them. To protect themselves they probably either lashed out with their long whiplike tails or stood on their rear legs and came crashing down onto an enemy with their front legs.

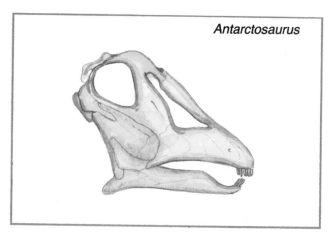

Antarctosaurus

The head was very small for the body, measuring only 24 inches (60 centimeters) in length. No complete skeletons of Antarctosaurus have been found. Much of the information we have about the creature is guesswork based on the bones and parts of the skeleton discovered.

Antarctosaurus means "not northern lizard." This animal belonged to the titanosaurids and was probably one of the largest dinosaurs. One thighbone was about 7.6 feet (2.3 meters) in length.

Weight not known
Length 60 feet (18 meters)
Found Brazil; Argentina; Uruguay; India; Kazakhstan, USSR
Lived Late Cretaceous

Apatosaurus

Apatosaurus means "deceptive lizard" or "headless lizard," and is the dinosaur which most people know as Brontosaurus.

Apatosaurus was a sauropod and belonged to the diplodocids. As far as we know, these dinosaurs were the longest ever to live on the Earth. Some of them were longer than a tennis court. Yet in spite of their length they were very light creatures. Some of them weighed only half as much as dinosaurs which were half their length.

The most noticeable features of the diplodocids were the long neck and the long tail. The nostrils consisted of a single hole midway between the eyes on the top of the skull.

Apatosaurus probably roamed in herds, wandering widely through swamps and over plains where forests grew. Scientists think it may have spent some of its time in shallow water.

The teeth were tiny and peglike, suitable for chewing leaves and stems. The animals might have moved about in family groups, with the younger ones in the middle for protection.

Weight 29 US tons (30 tonnes)
Length 65 feet (20 meters)
Found California, Utah, Oklahoma, and
Wyoming, USA
Lived Late Jurassic

Apatosaurus

Avimimus

Avimimus

Avimimus belonged to a group of dinosaurs called avimimids, which means "bird mimics." This name was given to the animals because they were very birdlike.

The first avimimid fossils were found by a Russian. When he made a list of their characteristics he was able to note down more than twenty features which were like those found on birds. Archaeopteryx, the earliest bird, still possessed feathers which were absent on Avimimus. Avimimids came later than Archaeopteryx.

However, from studing the fossils some scientists are convinced that Avimimus had wings with feathers on them. But closer study of the wings showed that the bird was unlikely to have used them for flight because they were very weak.

What the dinosaur lacked in flight power it made up for in speed. It could run extremely quickly, moving across the Mongolian plains where its remains were found. It is likely that it used its weak wings to lift itself briefly off the ground when it wanted to catch insects, which scientists think made up much of its diet.

The dinosaur had long, powerful leg bones, at the ends of which were feet similar to those of modern birds. Wings have not been discovered intact, but experts think that the dinosaur ran with them held close to the body.

Avimimus had large eyes which gave it a good view of things while it was moving along. One other interesting feature of this small animal was its large brain.

Weight not known
Length 5 feet (1.5 meters)
Found southern Mongolia
Lived Late Cretaceous

Bagaceratops

Bagaceratops belonged to the group of dinosaurs called ceratopsians, the "horned-faced lizards." The best known member of the group was Protoceratops.

Ceratopsians are divided into a number of groups and Bagaceratops is known as a protoceratopsid. Many of the animals in this group have been discovered in Mongolia, although others have been found in various places in North America.

The earliest of the ceratopsians included the agile Psittacosaurus. A dominant feature at the end of the head was a "parrot's beak."

Bagaceratops, or "small horned face", measured only 39 inches (1 meter) in length. Its neck was covered with a small frill and its snout had a small but distinctive horn. As in other ceratopsians, the head ended in a beak which had no teeth. Scientists think that this beak evolved to make it easier for the dinosaur to eat leaves. It was suitable for nipping off some of the thinner branches and twigs, as well as leaves.

Weight not known
Length 39 inches (1 meter)
Found Mongolia
Lived Late Cretaceous

Barosaurus

Barosaurus was a member of the group known as diplodocids, a name which means "double beam." Barosaurus means "heavy lizard." The most amazing thing about this group of dinosaurs is that in spite of their extremely large size they were quite light in weight. It has been calculated that Barosaurus was anything up to 90 feet (27.5 meters) in length, which is the same as placing more than fifteen adults head to toe. The bones in the body were large. Each of the bones in the neck was more than 39 inches (1 meter) in length.

Scientists have discovered this particular species in America and Tanzania. They were excited to find Barosaurus fossils from quite different parts of the world occurring in rocks of the same age.

Barosaurus

At one time, when land masses were linked and not separated by the sea as they are today, Barosaurus would have been able to move freely from one part of the world to another.

Barosaurus had a long neck rather like a giraffe's, and may have fed on leaves which it cropped from high up in the trees.

Weight not known
Length 72 – 90 feet (22 – 27 meters)
Found Tanzania; South Dakota and Wyoming, USA
Lived Late Jurassic

Brachiosaurus

Brachiosaurus was a sauropod and belonged to the group called brachiosaurids, after which it is named. The word brachiosaurid means "arm lizard," a name which comes from the dinosaur's long front limbs. These were longer than the back ones.

Research suggests that Brachiosaurus's relative was Cetiosauriscus, although they developed their own distinctive features. Brachiosaurus had a much longer neck, the longer arms already mentioned, and higher shoulders.

Brachiosaurus has so far been called the largest dinosaur ever to walk on the Earth, although bones from "Ultrasaurus" may show that it was a bigger creature. Fossil remains show that Brachiosaurus is taller than any other dinosaur. It is possible that others stood higher, but only Brachiosaurus has a complete skeleton to measure.

Many of the original theories about dinosaurs have changed. At one time it was suggested that the reason Brachiosaurus had nostrils on its head was so that the creature could breathe when the rest of the body was submerged in water. However, it is now thought that if Brachiosaurus had submerged itself, the weight of the water would have crushed its body.

Brachiosaurus did not have a heavy skull, which would have been too much weight for a long neck. Instead, the skull was very light. In some creatures trunks extend from the nasal openings, so it is possible that Brachiosaurus had a trunk. Another theory is that the skin inside these nostrils would have kept the dinosaur's brain cool in hot weather.

Weight 85 – 112 US tons (86 – 102 tonnes)
Length 75 – 90 feet (23 – 27 meters)
Found Algeria; Colorado, USA; Tanzania
Lived Late Jurassic

Brachiosaurus

Brachyceratops

Scientists are not in agreement about this particular dinosaur. So far, five or six skeletons have been found and all of them are from young animals. It has been suggested that Brachyceratops might even be a young Monoclonius, although no one has been able to prove this.

Brachyceratops was a ceratopsian and belonged to the group of short-frilled ceratopsids. These creatures have been separated from the long-frilled ceratopsids because the frill length is shorter.

Brachyceratops means "short horned face." It was only a small ceratopsian, measuring less

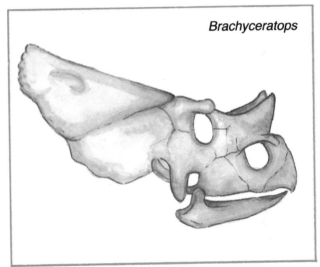

Brachyceratops

than 6 feet 6 inches (2 meters) in length. One feature of the creature's snout was a small, but well-developed, curved horn, with smaller horn-like features above each of the eyes. A short frill was present. So far all species of ceratopsids have been discovered in North America.

The toes of these creatures were hoofed, much like modern cattle. They were often compared with cattle because of their stocky body and plant-eating habits. They must also have been able to fend for themselves when threatened by flesh-eating carnosaurs.

Weight not known
Length 6 feet (1.8 meters)
Found Alberta, Canada; Montana, USA
Lived Late Cretaceous

Camarasaurus

Camarasaurus

Camarasaurus was a sauropod and gives its name to the group known as camarasaurids. The family name means "chambered lizards" and was given to these creatures because of a number of hollow spaces found in the backbone. Camarasaurids also had a long tail and neck, although both were shorter than in many of the sauropod relatives.

The large head of Camarasaurus held no fewer than forty-eight teeth, which were used for biting off plants.

Many young skeletons have been found, and these show how changes took place between the young and adult stage.

The top of the Camarasaurus skull shows some large nasal openings, and it is possible that the creature had a trunk.

Weight 20 US tons (18 tonnes)
Length 60 feet (18 meters)
Found Colorado, Oklahoma, Utah, and Wyoming, USA
Lived Late Jurassic

Camptosaurus

Camptosaurus gives its name to a family of dinosaurs known as the camptosaurids. The name means "bent lizard."

The jaws of Camptosaurus are interesting because they contain more teeth than are found in a simpler dinosaur such as Hypsilophodon. Very recently it has been discovered that Camptosaurus had a spike-shaped thumb similar to that of Iguanodon.

Footprints of the camptosaurids have been preserved in rocks, and a study of these has shown that the creatures may have walked on all four legs. The curved thighbone is how the family gets its name.

Weight 850 – 1100 pounds (380 – 500 kilograms)
Length 4 – 23 feet (1.2 – 7 meters)
Found western USA, western Europe
Lived Late Jurassic and Early Cretaceous

Camptosaurus

Ceratosaurus

Ceratosaurus

The ceratosaurids belong to the large group of flesh-eating dinosaurs. No one is quite certain about the ancestors, because only a few remains have been found so far.

We do know that they were all flesh-eating creatures. One peculiar feature of Ceratosaurus was a horn just above the nose. The male may have used this when searching out a mate or to warn other ceratosaurs of impending danger. The creatures also had distinct lumps above the eyes.

These dinosaurs were among the most savage creatures which ever roamed the Earth. They had extremely powerful jaws, vicious fanglike teeth, and efficient claws to grab and kill their prey.

Weight not known
Length 15 – 20 feet (4.6 – 6 meters)
Found Tanzania; Oklahoma, Colorado, and Utah, USA
Lived Late Jurassic

Cetiosauriscus

Bones of dinosaurs from the family of cetiosaurids – the "whale lizards" – were some of the first

Cetiosauriscus

Chasmosaurus

to be found. It was early in the last century, 1809, that the cetiosaurs were named from bones. It was because of the size of the bones that the people who discovered them thought that they belonged to some aquatic animal. More details of the size and shape of the creatures emerged when bones and teeth were discovered in 1841 and a partial skeleton was unearthed in Oxford later in the same century. They were obviously massive dinosaurs. Estimates show that even a small cetiosaurid could weigh as much as three Asian elephants.

A feature of the cetiosaurids was their heavily built backbone which, because of its length, added a great deal of weight to the skeleton. It was one of the first of the sauropods to evolve, and later creatures developed backbones which were much lighter.

The teeth of Cetiosauriscus were unusual. They were spoon-shaped and probably useful for grinding up the leaves on which the creature fed.

A skeleton discovered in Morocco in 1979 had a thighbone measuring 79 inches (200 centimeters) in length.

Weight 10 – 13 US tons (9 – 12 tonnes)
Length 45 – 60 feet (14 – 18 meters)
Found North America, Europe
Lived Middle to Late Jurassic

Chasmosaurus

Chasmosaurus, the "cleft lizard," was a ceratopsian dinosaur and belonged to the family of long-frilled ceratopsids. To date, it is the oldest long-frilled dinosaur to be found.

The long frill consisted of bone. Studies of Chasmosaurus have shown that this frill is very thin and is further lightened by the presence of holes. The frill may have helped to protect this plant-eating dinosaur, especially when it was attacked by the powerful Tyrannosaurus. But it is more likely that the frill was used for display.

Weight not known
Length 17 feet (5.2 meters)
Found Alberta, Canada; New Mexico, USA
Lived Late Cretaceous

Coelophysis

Coelophysis belonged to the group of dinosaurs known as coelurosaurs. Much of our knowledge about prehistoric animals has come from the study of only small parts of the skeleton or even of single bones. But large numbers of Coelophysis skeletons have been found. In several of the discoveries a number of the dinosaurs were close together. Some experts have suggested that it may have been some disaster which caused them to die this way.

Many hundreds of Coelophysis skeletons were found in a mass grave in New Mexico. This was fascinating to scientists because skeletons of different ages were found together.

Coelophysis was a small dinosaur and must have been able to move quickly, probably on two legs. Strong claws on the hands would have been used by the animal to strip flesh from large creatures, perhaps after they were already dead. The creature may also have fed on eggs, insects, and possibly lizards and small dinosaurs. The sharp, sawlike teeth were contained in a narrow skull.

Inside some of the skeletons were found the bones of other creatures of the same kind. At first, scientists suggested that these were young ready to be born. Now this has almost been ruled out because the bones are too big. So it is possible that the Coelophysis ate its own kind.

Weight 65 pounds (29.5 kilograms) max.
Length 10 feet (3 meters) max.
Found Massachusetts and New Mexico, USA
Lived Late Triassic

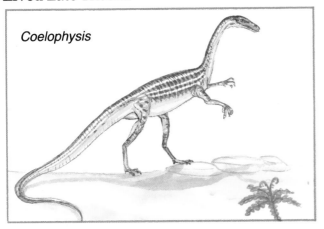
Coelophysis

Coelurus

The family of coelurids, to which Coelurus belonged, lived in different parts of the world. Coelurus means "hollow tail."

It is thought that these creatures lived by both hunting and scavenging. All of the group were small dinosaurs, the largest probably only slightly bigger than a man. The smallest was about the size of a goose.

A study of the limb bones shows that the hind legs had special joints at the ankle. These allowed the dinosaur to move quickly. The creature's light weight also helped it to move quickly. The bones of the backbone, or vertebrae, were hollow and made the skeleton lighter. The head of Coelurus is small enough to be held in a man's hand.

Coelurus

Although Coelurus was only a small dinosaur, its fingers were large enough to pick up small creatures for food. It would have seized them as it moved over the plant-covered land. Two of the three fingers had sharp claws. Lizards probably formed the major part of the dinosaur's diet, but it may also have taken small pterosaurs.

Weight 50 pounds (22.5 kilograms)
Length 6 feet 6 inches (2 meters)
Found Wyoming, USA
Lived Late Cretaceous

Compsognathus

Compsognathus was a member of the coelurosaurs, or "hollow-tailed lizards." The family of compsognathids falls within the group of coelurosaurs and its name means "pretty jaw." These creatures are some of the smallest dinosaurs to have been discovered.

Compsognathus was the size of a hen, with a long tail and neck. It was a swift hunter. The remains of a lizard have been found inside the body of one skeleton.

From the materials first uncovered it was thought that Compsognathus had flippers, but this is no longer thought to have been possible.

Weight 6 pounds 8 ounces (3 kilograms)
Length 2 feet (60 centimeters)
Found southeastern France,
 southern Germany
Lived Late Jurassic

Compsognathus

Corythosaurus

Daspletosaurus

Corythosaurus

Corythosaurus was a hadrosaurid, or "duck-bill" dinosaur. At the front of the head was a toothless bill, similar to a duck's bill, with the rest of the jaw containing large numbers of grinding teeth.

Corythosaurus was the "helmet lizard" because of the distinctive tall, narrow, hollow crest on the head. Females and young may have had only small helmets.

Hadrosaurids ate tough plants including twigs as well as fruits and seeds. Preserved stomach contents have revealed their eating habits.

The nasal passage went up the snout and curved around back into the mouth. Perhaps Corythosaurus used these for making elephant-like calls to others of its species.

Weight 4.2 US tons (3.8 tonnes)
Length 33 feet (10 meters)
Found Montana, USA; Alberta, Canada
Lived Late Cretaceous

Daspletosaurus

The family of tyrannosaurids, of which the most famous was Tyrannosaurus, included Daspleto-saurus. The tyrannosaurids have been called the "terrible lizards" because at one time research seemed to suggest that they were vicious killers.

Daspletosaurus was the "frightful lizard," with a head as large as that of Tyrannosaurus and equally vicious teeth. Having such large and powerful teeth, these dinosaurs may have been able to attack and kill the heavily plated animals.

Weight 4 US tons (3.6 tonnes)
Length 28 feet (8.5 meters)
Found Alberta, Canada
Lived Late Cretaceous

Deinocheirus

The discovery of fossil remains of Deinocheirus, or "terrible hand," has left scientists puzzled. The two hands and arms which have been recovered measure nearly 9 feet (2.7 meters) in length. Comparisons with other dinosaur remains show that the arms were longer than those of the "scythe lizards" (such as Therizino-saurus), although they were thinner and less powerful.

No one knows what Deinocheirus was like, but it was probably large and lightly built. With claws of 12 inches (30 centimeters) in length, it could have been a meat-eater.

Weight not known
Length arm bones 8 feet 6 inches (2.6 meters)
Found southern Mongolia
Lived Late Cretaceous

Deinocheirus

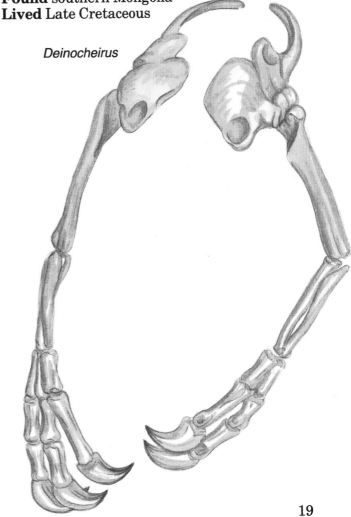

D

Deinonychus

Until the dromaeosaurids were discovered, experts thought that most dinosaurs were slow-moving creatures. But the dromaeosaurids, to which Deinonychus belonged, are known as the "running lizards," and were vicious killers.

Deinonychus had hands with three fingers, and these, together with an extremely large and powerful sickle-shaped claw on the second toe, enabled the dinosaur to deal efficiently with plant-eating animals.

Deinonychus, known as "terrible claw," was the largest of the dromaeosaurids. From well-preserved skeletons found in the United States, it has been possible to build up a good picture of the creature.

Another feature of the family was the stiff tail. Bony rods growing out around the tail meant that it could be held out behind the body. The dinosaur may have stood on one leg when attacking its prey. If it did, the tail would have helped it to balance more easily.

Dinosaurs within this family each had a large brain to control the body. Deinonychus was light and agile. When moving quickly it may have used its shorter toes for running, holding the claw in a backward position.

Weight not known
Length 8 – 13 feet (2.4 – 4 meters)
Found western USA
Lived Early Cretaceous

Deinonychus

Dicraeosaurus

Dicraeosaurus was a member of the diplodocid family, which included better-known dinosaurs like Apatosaurus and Diplodocus (from which the family gets its name). This family of dinosaurs had extremely long necks and tails. Some of its members are the largest dinosaurs ever discovered. Long, overlapping spines gave extra support to the neck.

Like its relatives, Dicraeosaurus seemed to favor areas with plenty of plant cover. As with many other early observations, those about the sauropods were incorrect. The first conclusions were that these animals would have been able to survive only if they lived in water, which would have supported the massive bulk of the body.

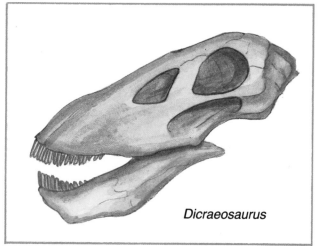
Dicraeosaurus

Later investigations suggest that the sauropods lived on land.

Dicraeosaurus was the "forked lizard," so named because of large extensions of the vertebrae making up the back. An examination of these bones showed that they were Y-shaped, rather like forks.

It is strange that such large creatures should have had such weak jaws. The few teeth that were found were only in the front part of the mouth.

Weight not known
Length 43 – 66 feet (13 – 20 meters)
Found Tanzania
Lived Late Jurassic

Dilophosaurus

Dilophosaurus was a carnosaur and, like many of its relatives, it was a large flesh-eating dinosaur.

These creatures walked upright on their long rear limbs. The front limbs were shorter, although quite strong and well developed. It is difficult to tell how these creatures captured and killed their food. They may have used their strong limbs to attack unsuspecting animals. They would have held on to their prey with the three long claws on the hand. They would then have sunk their large teeth into the flesh, tearing it apart and crushing the bones.

Dilophosaurus is the oldest of the meat-eating dinosaurs so far discovered, and only a few remains have been found. The name Dilophosaurus means "two-ridged lizard," because of the strange bony ridges on the creature's head. There were two of these thin, fragile crests, but it is not known whether they were found on both males and females. These crests were for display and may have been brightly colored.

Weight not known
Length at least 20 feet (6 meters)
Found Arizona, USA
Lived Early Jurassic

Diplodocus

Diplodocus means "double beam," a name which derives from the pieces of bone projecting from the backbone of the dinosaur. The tail consisted of seventy vertebrae. There were ten vertebrae in the back and fifteen in the neck.

Diplodocus was one of the largest dinosaurs to live on the Earth but it was not the heaviest. It was slimly built with a long, thin neck and whiplash tail. On a modern tennis court the creature would stretch from end to end.

Diplodocus had extremely sturdy legs which it needed to support its large body. Reconstructions of the skeletons show that the front legs were shorter than the back ones. This probably means that the creature's back sloped upward from the neck and that it was higher at the thighs than anywhere else.

On the inner toes of the front feet were strong claws. No one knows for certain why they were

Dilophosaurus

Diplodocus

Dromaeosaurus

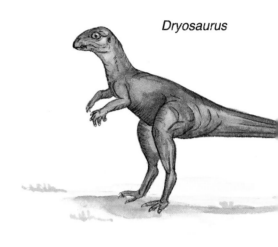

Dryosaurus

there, but Diplodocus probably used them to defend itself.

Inside the jaw were thin, pencillike teeth which occurred only at the front of the mouth. Because the teeth were so weak, the animal would have had to be content with a diet of leaves and other low-growing vegetation. The plants which were swallowed whole were ground up in the stomach, probably with the help of pebbles which the animal had previously swallowed.

Weight 11.7 US tons (10.6 tonnes)
Length 87 feet 6 inches (27 meters)
Found USA
Lived Late Jurassic

Dromaeosaurus

Although only a small creature, Dromaeosaurus was an extremely vicious meat-eater. This dinosaur gave its name to the family of dromaeosaurids, the well-known "running lizards." It was this group of dinosaurs which created a great deal of excitement when the first relatively complete remains were found in the 1960s.

Dromaeosaurus was very agile and capable of pouncing on other creatures. It had exceptionally sharp claws on each of the second toes and would have used them to grip the prey, and then to tear apart the flesh.

These long claws did not get in the way when the dinosaur walked because they were pivoted and could be carried in an upright position. Dromaeosaurus was also able to swing the claws from side to side, which was useful for striking an enemy.

So far, no complete skeleton of the creature has been found. Details of the animal have been built up from remains consisting of some bones and a skull.

Weight not known
Length 8 – 13 feet (2.4 – 4 meters)
Found southern Alberta, Canada
Lived Late Cretaceous

Dryosaurus

Dryosaurus belonged to the group of ornithopods, or "bird feet" dinosaurs. These creatures were able to run in an upright position on their hind legs.

The skeletons of these dinosaurs have been compared with the bones of our modern deer, which are swift-moving, browsing animals. There are many similarities.

The ornithopods evolved over millions of years and changed from being quite small animals to much larger ones. Dryosaurus was one of the larger members of the family of hypsilophodontids. The front of the mouth was beak-

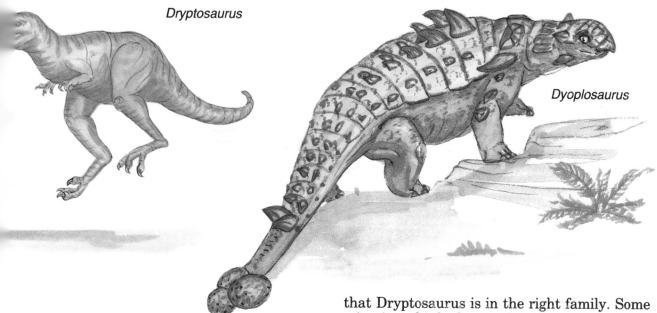

Dryptosaurus

Dyoplosaurus

like without any teeth. Dryosaurus used this beak to bite off plant leaves. Once the food had been collected, it was then pushed to the back of the mouth where the "high ridge teeth" ground up the material so that it could be swallowed easily. It is from the high ridge teeth that the family gets the name hypsilophodontids.

These creatures are now thought to be among the speediest of the animals which lived during the Age of Reptiles.

Weight not known
Length 9 – 14 feet (2.7 – 4.3 meters)
Found eastern England, Romania, Tanzania, western states of the USA
Lived Middle to Late Jurassic

Dryptosaurus

Because so few bones of Dryptosaurus have been found, no one is quite sure what it looked like. With so few remains it has not been possible to build up a complete skeleton.

The dryptosaurids are known as the "wounding lizards." The family has been given this name because it seems certain that its members were powerful animals. Not everyone agrees

that Dryptosaurus is in the right family. Some scientists think that it should be in the same family as Tyrannosaurus.

The bones of Dryptosaurus have been recovered in North America. A bone found in Mongolia may also belong to the same family.

When the American fossil collector E. D. Cope discovered Dryptosaurus bones, he called the creature "Laelaps," which means "the leaper." Cope's initial study of the skeleton, which he found in 1866, led him to believe that the dinosaur moved like a kangaroo. He assumed that the animal had very large hind limbs and could bound like a kangaroo in order to land on its prey. Digging the sharp claws on its hind feet into the food, it would then have torn the flesh apart.

Weight not known
Length more than 20 feet (6 meters)
Found North America
Lived Late Cretaceous

Dyoplosaurus

To some scientists Dyoplosaurus and Euoplocephalus are the same dinosaur. But there are other people who think that Euoplocephalus is a different creature, although closely related to Dyoplosaurus.

Dyoplosaurus was an ankylosaur. These creatures varied in size from that of a bus to an average-sized man. Although ankylosaurs were very well-built dinosaurs they had very small teeth. This meant that these dinosaurs could have eaten only soft material such as plants or insects. No one is certain.

The large ankylosaurs were well-protected and able to survive attacks from the vicious meat-eating animals. Dyoplosaurus means "double-armored lizard" and Euoplocephalus means "well-armored head." This part of the skeleton was more than 14 inches (35 centimeters) across. The body skin had a number of bony plates, spines, and shields, providing good protection against the sharp teeth of the carnosaurs.

Dyoplosaurus had a heavy club near the end of its tail which it could swing when attacking its enemies.

Weight 2 – 3 US tons (2.7 tonnes)
Length 23 feet (7 meters)
Found Alberta, Canada; possibly Sinkiang, northwest China
Lived Late Cretaceous

Edmontosaurus

Edmontosaurus was a hadrosaurid, or "duckbill" dinosaur, so called because of the toothless beak at the front of the head. People who studied the first hadrosaurids had difficulty. They took it for granted that the head had weak teeth in it. But later skulls were easier to look at and careful examination showed that the teeth were farther back in the mouth.

Duckbill dinosaurs were supposed to have fed like ducks in muddy ponds and marshy areas. Here, they apparently used their beaks like ducks. However some hadrosaurids weighed between 2 and 3 tons (2 and 3 tonnes), and it is difficult imagining them feeding in the same way as ducks!

The hard beak, made of a horny material, probably grew throughout the dinosaur's life. Hadrosaurids probably used their tough bills to strip leaves from trees and to cut off twigs.

The fossils of some hadrosaurids have been found complete with their stomach contents. These fossil remains, now in a West German museum, showed that the dinosaur had eaten seeds, twigs, and pine needles, as well as other prehistoric plants.

After many arguments it is now thought that hadrosaurids moved their jaws up and down so that the teeth moved against each other. As the tooth material wore away, it produced a rough surface.

A hadrosaurid nest was discovered in 1978 in western Montana, and fossil skeletons were also unearthed. The discovery of the nest, eggs, and young dinosaurs revealed a great deal. When the teeth of the young dinosaurs were examined they were found to be worn. These youngsters were larger than the newly hatched dinosaurs. Although no one can be sure what happened, it is possible that the young dinosaurs remained with their parents for some time. Perhaps they stayed close to the nest to be brought food by the adults; or perhaps they went out in search of their own food and then returned to the nest for protection.

Edmontosaurus skeletons have been found and the dinosaur has been carefully studied. It

Edmontosaurus

is now known that Edmontosaurus and a dinosaur called Anatosaurus, which was thought to be a different creature, are one and the same.

Edmontosaurus was one of the largest of the duckbill dinosaurs. It measured nearly 42.5 feet (13 meters) in length. The skull was low at the front and high at the back. Hollowing around the nasal openings may indicate that the creature had a fleshy snout.

Weight 2.9 – 3.9 US tons (3 – 4 tonnes)
Length 42 feet 6 inches (13 meters)
Found New Jersey and Montana, USA; Alberta, Canada
Lived Late Cretaceous

Elaphrosaurus

Elaphrosaurus was the oldest of the group of dinosaurs known as ornithomimids. Elaphrosaurus had short arms and legs when compared with later ostrich dinosaurs, which suggests that it could not move as quickly as they could.

A comparison of the skeleton of Elaphrosaurus and a modern-day ostrich shows many similarities. But instead of having a feathered wing, the dinosaur had clawed hands.

Like its other relatives, Elaphrosaurus had powerful legs, enabling it to move along quickly. It had a narrow tail which it held out straight for balance.

Elaphrosaurus

At the end of the long neck there was a rather small head. This was light in weight because the bones were thin and delicate. There were no teeth in the head.

Elaphrosaurus means "light lizard." Skeletons of these creatures were found in a famous dinosaur area known as the Tendaguru Dino-

saur Beds in Tanzania. Other dinosaurs like Barosaurus, Brachiosaurus, and Kentrosaurus lived in the same area.

Weight not known
Length 11 feet 6 inches (3.5 meters)
Found Tanzania, Algeria, Tunisia, Morocco, Egypt
Lived Late Jurassic and Early Cretaceous

Euhelopus

Euhelopus, or "good marsh foot," was a member of the group of sauropod dinosaurs known as camarasaurids. Although they were large creatures, they were lighter than some other dinosaurs of the same size because they had hollow areas in their backbone. This feature gives the group their name "chambered lizards."

Although extremely large, these dinosaurs spent their lives feeding on plants. Fossils which have been discovered show that the sauropods were the largest-ever land creatures.

The body was supported by four thick legs. At the end of the extremely long neck was a small

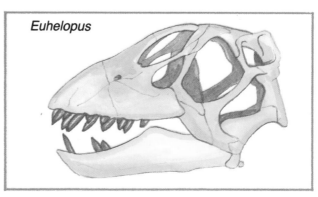
Euhelopus

head. Special arrangements of muscles and ligaments enabled the dinosaur to lift its head up and down and from side to side.

Nasal openings on the top of the head of Euhelopus have puzzled scientists. It is possible that the creature had a trunk.

Weight up to 27 US tons (24 tonnes)
Length 33 – 50 feet (10 – 15 meters)
Found Shantung, eastern China
Lived Early Cretaceous

Euskelosaurus

Euskelosaurus was one of the first dinosaurs to be found in Africa. It is a prosauropod, which means "before the lizard feet." The group used to be known as the paleopods, which means "old feet." Euskelosaurus means "well-limbed lizard."

The dinosaur belonged to a family known as plateosaurids, or "flat lizards." The legs of these particular animals were probably arranged slightly to one side of the body. Because so few bones have been found it is not possible to tell exactly how the creature was built.

The dinosaur's diet consisted of plants.

Weight 2 US tons (1.8 tonnes)
Length 40 feet (12 meters)
Found South Africa
Lived Late Triassic to Early Jurassic

Fabrosaurus

Fabrosaurus means "Fabre's lizard." It was a small dinosaur standing no more than 39 inches (1 meter) in height. It had long, strong hind limbs, so that it could run well.

Fabrosaurus had strong teeth and could eat tough vegetation. Holes in the jaw suggest that perhaps new teeth grew to replace those which wore out.

Weight not known
Length 3 feet 3 inches (1 meter)
Found Lesotho, Africa
Lived Late Triassic to Early Jurassic

Euskelosaurus

Fabrosaurus

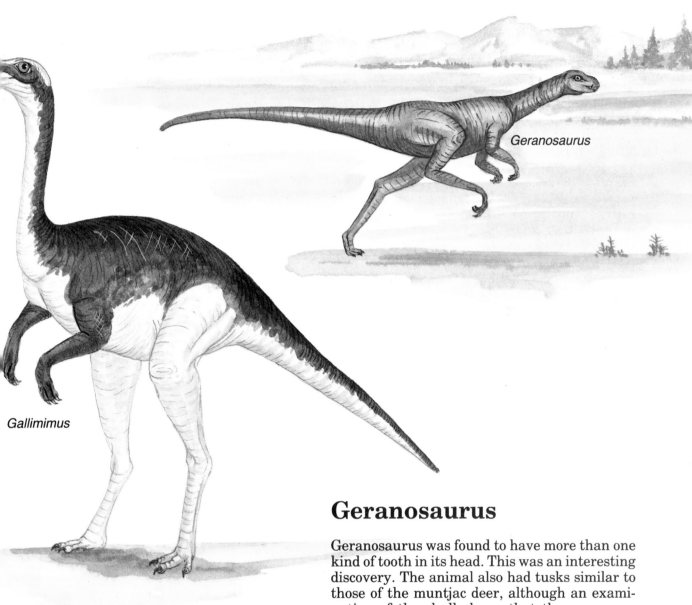

Geranosaurus

Gallimimus

Gallimimus

Gallimimus, known as "hen mimic," was probably the largest of the ostrich dinosaurs. These animals may have had difficulty picking things up, and may have fed by scraping away the soil to get at dinosaur eggs.

Weight not known
Length 13 feet (4 meters)
Found southern Mongolia
Lived Late Cretaceous

Geranosaurus

Geranosaurus was found to have more than one kind of tooth in its head. This was an interesting discovery. The animal also had tusks similar to those of the muntjac deer, although an examination of the skull shows that there were no suitable sockets for these tusks.

Geranosaurus, which means "crane lizard," is not very well-known. To date only a few bones have been found, along with pieces of the animal's jaws. It is thought that the teeth at the front of the skull could lop off pieces of plants. Those at the back were then used for grinding the food.

Weight not known
Length 47 inches (1.2 meters)
Found Cape Province, South Africa
Lived Late Triassic/Early Jurassic

Hadrosaurus

Hadrosaurus gives its name to the group known as hadrosaurids, or the "duckbills" – a name chosen because they had beaks similar to those of our present-day ducks (see Edmontosaurus). Duckbill dinosaurs show a great variation in size, from those as small as a man to others as large as an elephant.

The first duckbill dinosaurs may have appeared in Asia. They gradually spread into Europe and across South America. In North America they were very numerous and may have been the most common of the North American dinosaurs. Large numbers of fossils have been unearthed.

Hadrosaurus, "big lizard," was one of the first complete dinosaur skeletons to be discovered and named in North America.

Weight not known
Length 26 – 33 feet (8 – 10 meters)
Found New Jersey, USA; Mexico; Alberta, Canada
Lived Late Cretaceous

Hadrosaurus

Halticosaurus

Halticosaurus was one of the largest of the coelurosaurs, a group of dinosaurs with hollow bones. These flesh-eating animals were quite small. Their remains suggest that they were lightly built, with long legs enabling them to run quickly.

Coelurosaurs had hands with sharp claws on each of the five fingers. The toes also had sharp

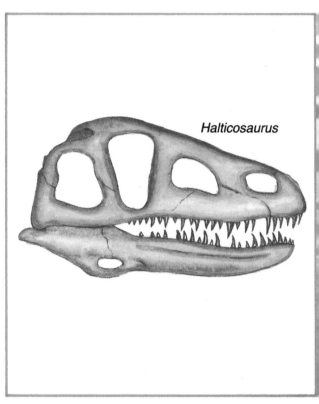
Halticosaurus

claws. Coelurosaurs used these claws for removing the flesh from dead animals, and they probably ate young dinosaurs as well as eggs and insects. Inside the skull of Halticosaurus there were sharp teeth, ideal for eating meat.

The only remains found so far of Halticosaurus – the "nimble lizard" – were unearthed in Germany. A skeleton and two skulls were found.

Weight not known
Length 18 feet (5.5 meters)
Found southern Germany
Lived Late Triassic

Hylaeosaurus

Hylaeosaurus was the "woodland lizard" and was one of the armored ankylosaurs. The barrel-shaped bodies of the various species had a strange assortment of projections sticking out from the body. With spikes and spines, as well as "armor plating," the creatures were well protected against meat-eating dinosaurs. The small teeth of Hylaeosaurus were suited only for plants.

Hylaeosaurus was one of the earliest dinosaurs to be discovered, and the first nodosaurid. It was found in Sussex in southern England in 1833.

The remains were incomplete, consisting of the front half of the skeleton without the skull. The bones of the skeleton are still partly embedded in the block of limestone in which they were fossilized.

Weight not known
Length 20 feet (6 meters)
Found southern England
Lived Early Cretaceous

Hylaeosaurus

Hypacrosaurus

Hypacrosaurus was another of the "duckbill" dinosaurs. It belongs to the family known as lambeosaurine duckbills. These are "Lambe's lizards," and Hypacrosaurus means "below the top lizard." The main feature of these dinosaurs was a large crest which grew out from the top of the head. Males may have had the largest crests. Females and young dinosaurs may have had smaller ones.

Hypacrosaurus

The crest on the skull of Hypacrosaurus was shorter than on other duckbills such as Corythosaurus. The crest was round in outline and was formed when skull bones grew outward and backward, ending in a spike at the rear of the head. Large numbers of strong teeth provided a good area for grinding up plants. This constant action would have worn down the teeth, and when they fell out new ones would have replaced them.

Weight not known
Length 30 feet (9 meters)
Found Montana, USA; Alberta, Canada
Lived Late Cretaceous

Hypselosaurus

Hypselosaurus was a sauropod related to Alamosaurus. When the first sauropods were discovered, no information was known about how they gave birth. Later, when nests and eggs were discovered, scientists concluded that sauropods and other dinosaurs laid eggs and did not give birth to live young. But one puzzling question remained: How could such large animals lay eggs without crushing them?

Eggs laid by a female Hypelosaurus have been found in Aix-en-Provence, France. The regular arrangement of the eggs suggests that they were laid while the dinosaur was close to the ground. Dinosaurs were careful enough not to step on their egg nests.

The eggs measure about 12 inches (30 centimeters) long and 10 inches (25 centimeters) wide, but are quite small in relation to the creature which laid them. Larger eggs would have needed thicker shells, and then the young dinosaurs would not have been able to get out, or to get enough air while inside.

Hypselosaurus was the "high ridge lizard," and it belonged to the titanosaurids. Although this word means "giant lizards," not all the members were large. Also, at least one titanosaurid had small armor plates, which have not been found on other sauropods.

Like other titanosaurids, Hypselosaurus had a long tail. The head was short and there were weak, peglike teeth in the jaws.

Weight not known
Length 40 feet (12 meters)
Found France, Spain
Lived Late Cretaceous

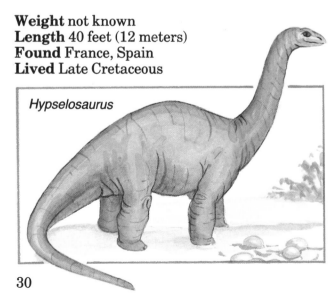
Hypselosaurus

Hypsilophodon

When the first remains of Hypsilophodon were found it was thought that this dinosaur climbed trees, because the smallest of the four toes appeared to point backward, allowing the creature to hold on to branches. More careful studies of the feet showed that all the toes pointed forward.

Hypsilophodon belonged to the hypsilophodontids, a group of lightly built dinosaurs which could run very fast. They are often called the gazelles of the dinosaur world. Careful studies of

Hypsilophodon

the creature's legs have shown that the shinbones were long and the thighbones shorter. This is how the legs of fast-running animals are built. The stiff tail helped Hypsilophodon to balance when it was running fast.

As far as we know, hypsilophodontids lived on Earth for about one hundred million years, longer than any other family of dinosaurs.

Hypsilophodon had a large number of teeth in its jaws for chewing plants. The teeth wore down because they were in constant use, but new teeth replaced them.

Weight not known
Length 4 feet 6 inches to 7 feet 6 inches
   (1.4 – 2.3 meters)
Found southern England
Lived Early Cretaceous

Iguanodon

Iguanodon, or "iguana tooth," was an iguanodontid. Members of the iguanodontid family ranged from about 16 to 33 feet (4.8 to 10 meters) in length. The larger ones could stand as tall as a modern elephant.

Iguanodon is the best-known member of this family. It was also the largest. Although the creature could probably stand upright, it also walked on all fours. Discoveries in the United States show large footprints for the hind feet and smaller ones for the front feet.

This creature probably roamed in herds of various sizes. It is impossible to tell the males from the females.

No one is quite sure what the creature's thumb spikes were for, but they may have been used to pull down branches. The thumb might also have been used for defense.

Weight 5 US tons (4.5 tonnes)
Length 29.5 feet (9 meters)
Found western Europe, Mongolia, North Africa, western North America
Lived Early Cretaceous

Ischisaurus

Ischisaurus was one of the earliest dinosaurs. Not much is known about it because only partial skeletons, including parts of the leg and skull, have so far been discovered. Researchers have studied these fossilized remains and think that these dinosaurs may have been the ancestors of the better-known sauropods.

Ischisaurus belonged to the family called herrerasaurids. Creatures in this group were reptiles with sharp teeth. The "Ischigulasto lizard" gets its name from the Ischigulasto rock formations in northwest Argentina. Each of the creature's teeth was shaped like a sickle.

Weight not known
Length 7 feet (2 meters)
Found northwest Argentina
Lived Late Triassic

Ischisaurus

Iguanodon

Kentrosaurus

Kentrosaurus was a stegosaurid closely related to the well-known Stegosaurus. Like Stegosaurus, Kentrosaurus was covered with a number of bony projections. Those on the shoulders and neck were flat and platelike. Midway along the back the plates changed to narrow spines. One spinelike projection stuck out from the top of the thighs.

Weight not known
Length 16 feet (5 meters)
Found Tanzania
Lived Late Jurassic

Lambeosaurus

Lambeosaurus was a typical hadrosaurid, or "duckbill" dinosaur (see Edmontosaurus and Hadrosaurus). Many of the hadrosaurids had distinctive crests. On Lambeosaurus this was "hatchet-shaped," and a spine ran backward from it. A neck frill may have grown from this.

The nostrils on the snout opened by passages into the hollow crest. The reason for such large crests is not understood, although some people think that these features allowed the creatures to recognize others of their own kind.

Weight not known
Length 49 feet (15 meters)
Found Montana, USA; Alberta, Canada
Lived Late Cretaceous

Kentrosaurus

Lambeosaurus

Leptoceratops

Leptoceratops

Leptoceratops, or "slim horned face," belonged to the family known as protoceratopsids. It was a relative of the better known Protoceratops, but was much smaller, measuring only about 3 feet (1 meter) in length. This group of animals, together with the psittacosaurs, were some of the last dinosaurs to be found on the Earth.

Leptoceratops had front legs shorter than the back ones, but it probably remained on all fours.

There was no horn on the head of Leptoceratops. It was classified as a protoceratopsid because it had a short frill at the back of the skull. It has features which suggest that it is more closely related to the psitticosaurs.

Weight not known
Length 3 feet (1 meter)
Found Mongolia; Alberta, Canada; Wyoming, USA
Lived Late Cretaceous

L

Lexovisaurus

Lexovisaurus means "Lexovi lizard." It gets its name from the Lexovi tribe which lived in the northwest part of France. The bones of the dinosaur were first found there.

Lexovisaurus was one of the oldest stegosaurids. Only a few good remains have been unearthed, so we know less about this creature than about other stegosaurids. Most of the remains consist of pieces of armor and limb bones.

Lexovisaurus had a number of features like those of Kentrosaurus. Both had triangular plates on the neck, and spines on the back, hips, and tail. The plates were probably at their biggest in the middle of the dinosaur's back, gradually forming smaller spines which continued along the back and tail. A quick swing of the dinosaur's tail might well have dealt a nasty blow to an enemy.

Like the other stegosaurids, Lexovisaurus had small teeth which were well suited for feeding on leaves.

Weight not known
Length 17 feet (5 meters)
Found northwest France, southern England
Lived Middle Jurassic

Lufengosaurus

Lufengosaurus was a prosauropod dinosaur. These creatures were found over much of the world and all of them, from the smallest to the largest, relied on plants for their food.

Lufengosaurus belonged to the plateosaurids. This particular genus was found in China and is one of the oldest dinosaurs to come out of that country. Lufengosaurus means "Lufeng lizard," taking its name from its place of discovery, Lufeng, in the south of China.

Like other members of this family the creature had extremely large hands and broad feet which probably helped it to stand properly. The head was at the end of a relatively long neck and contained teeth which were long and narrow. The teeth had notched edges for cutting plants.

The creatures had long necks which helped them reach the higher branches of trees. Prosauropods were the first dinosaurs to be able to do this.

Weight not known
Length 20 feet (6 meters)
Found southern China
Lived Late Triassic or Early Jurassic

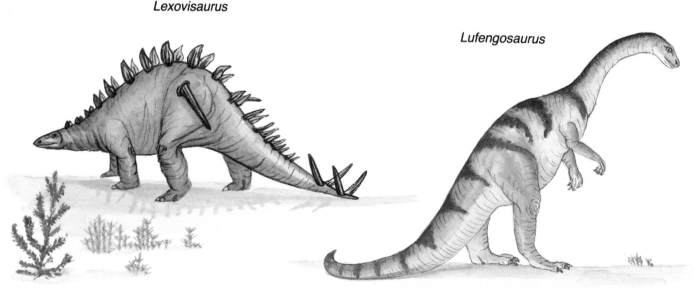

Lexovisaurus

Lufengosaurus

34

Lycorhinus

Lycorhinus was an ornithopod, a word which means "bird foot." These were among the bird-hipped (ornithischian) dinosaurs, which were able to walk and run on their hind legs.

Lycorhinus, or "wolf snout," belonged to a family of dinosaurs called heterodontosaurids, which means "different-toothed lizards."

When the first heterodontosaurids, like Lycorhinus, were discovered in southern Africa, one scientist thought that the creatures may have become inactive during part of the summer when temperatures were high and food was scarce. Another scientist contradicted him.

Because few remains of the dinosaur have been found we still do not know a great deal about it. The first remnant, which turned up in 1924, was part of the left cheekbone of Lycorhinus.

The creature's large canine tooth was similar to that of Heterodontosaurus, and the other teeth also bore some similarities. This fascinating dinosaur was not very big, the largest measuring less than 4 feet 10 inches (1.5 meters) in length.

Weight not known
Length 4 feet 10 inches (1.5 meters)
Found Cape Province, South Africa
Lived Late Triassic/Early Jurassic

Maiasaura

Maiasaura is one of the group known as hadrosaurid, or "duckbill" dinosaurs. This particular species belonged to the family of hadrosaurine duckbills. Nearly twenty species of these have so far been identified.

Maiasaura means "good mother lizard," a name given to it because of the recent finds. Fossilized baby dinosaurs were found around a mound-shaped nest. There were fifteen of these baby dinosaurs, each measuring about 39 inches (1 meter) in length. This find was very important because it told scientists that there were family arrangements in which the young dinosaurs remained by the nest after hatching.

Dinosaur nests are not discovered very often. The Maiasaura and Protoceratops nest finds are the most famous. The first discoveries were made in Montana. Great activity then led to more finds. Young dinosaurs measuring about 20 inches (50 centimeters) were unearthed. Other nests contained only shells. When the distance between nests was measured, it was found to be the same as the length of a fully grown adult.

The young may have died in the nest from starvation. Perhaps the adults were killed by their enemies while they were out collecting food for the young. We do not know.

Weight not known
Length 30 feet (9 meters)
Found Montana, USA
Lived Late Cretaceous

Lycorhinus

Maiasaura

M

Massospondylus

Massospondylus belonged to the group known as prosauropods. It was a plant-eater and lived over a wide area. Scientists are rather puzzled by this group of dinosaurs. They have been found on every continent except Antarctica. Remains are plentiful. Studies of Massospondylus, which means "massive vertebra," have shown how the creature dealt with its food. Pebbles in the stomach probably ground up the plant material so that it could be digested easily. These pebbles were very numerous and ground smooth from the active motion within the stomach.

Some backbones were found in South Africa, then brought to England where they were studied by the famous fossil collector Richard Owen.

On the first "thumb" of Massospondylus was a large claw that might have been pressed up against the other digits to grasp or hold objects.

Weight not known
Length 13 feet (4 meters)
Found southern Africa
Lived Late Triassic/Early Jurassic

Massospondylus

Megalosaurus

Megalosaurus is the "great lizard" and belonged to the group known as theropods. Like the other members of this group, Megalosaurus was a flesh-eating dinosaur.

The dinosaur had three very powerful claws on its toes and long claws on its hands. When a Megalosaurus went out hunting it probably swung out at its prey, using the sharp claws on its hands to grip the flesh. Once it had a creature in its grip, it would then have sunk its extremely large fangs into the unfortunate animal. The teeth and jaws of this dinosaur were so strong that it could easily tear flesh apart and crush bones as well.

Remains of Megalosaurus have been unearthed in Africa, Asia, Europe, and South America. A variety of bones and teeth have been discovered, as well as what are thought to be the creature's footprints. Around twenty different kinds of megalosaurid dinosaur have so far been identified. Studies of the rocks containing remains of Megalosaurus have puzzled scientists because it seems that the dinosaurs had been on the Earth for more than 100 million years. It may turn out that some of the very small finds have come from other creatures.

Weight 1 US ton (900 kilograms)
Length 30 feet (9 meters)
Found South America, Asia, Europe, and Africa
Lived Early Jurassic (perhaps) to
  Early Cretaceous

Megalosaurus

Melanorosaurus

Melanorosaurus was a prosauropod and is known as the "black lizard." Its relatives include Euskelosaurus and Plateosaurus.

Scientists cannot agree on whether Melanorosaurus and Euskelosaurus are one and the same or different. Although the animal has been placed in the plateosaurid family, the latest research seems to suggest that Melanorosaurus may end up in a group of its own called melanorosaurids.

Most of the remains of Melanorosaurus consist of rib bones uncovered in South Africa. Although not much of the skeleton has been found, experts think that Melanorosaurus was a large creature which moved around on all four limbs. Using bones from this animal and from its dinosaur relatives, scientists have been able to build up a picture of the creature.

Prosauropods probably evolved into big animals in order to be a match for their enemies. Because we do not have many remains, it is not possible to tell whether they had teeth like sauropods.

Weight 2 US tons (1.8 tonnes)
Length 40 feet (12.2 meters)
Found South Africa
Lived Late Triassic/Early Jurassic

Melanorosaurus

Monoclonius

Monoclonius was a ceratopsian, or "horned dinosaur." The first discoveries of this creature were made near the mouth of the Judith River in Montana, in 1855. Only a few teeth were unearthed, but they were identified as belonging to Monoclonious, the "one-horned dinosaur". In addition to the large horn which was found on the nose of this creature, there were raised areas above the eyes.

This short-frilled ceratopsid had scaly skin. Monoclonius had two rather large holes in the frill and bony knobs along its edge.

Nine short-frilled ceratopsids have been found, including the well-known Triceratops. Sometimes more than one species of the same creature is discovered.

Weight not known
Length 18 feet (5.5 meters)
Found Alberta, Canada; western USA
Lived Late Cretaceous

Monoclonius

Mussaurus

The bones of Mussaurus, called the "mouse lizard," were found in Argentina. It was of great interest to scientists because the bones were so small. No other remains of this creature have yet been found, and it is clear that these bones belonged to very young animals.

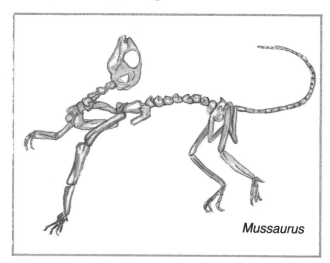

Mussaurus

Mussaurus was a prosauropod. The skeletons which were found were incomplete. They were discovered in Patagonia in the southern part of Argentina. One specimen was so small that the skeleton could easily be held in the human hand. The largest specimen was about 8 inches (20 centimeters). Two eggs belonging to the same dinosaur were also discovered. Young that were discovered in a nest with eggs may have been very young Mussaurus, although further research may show that they were the young of other dinosaurs.

Weight not known
Length 8 inches approx (20 centimeters)
Found Argentina
Lived Late Triassic

Muttaburrasaurus

Muttaburrasaurus is the "Muttaburra lizard," found near a place called Muttaburra in Queensland, Australia. The skeleton was discovered in 1981 and caused a great deal of excitement. So far we know very little about Australian dinosaurs because so few remains have been uncovered.

Although the skeleton was not very well preserved, scientists have been able to give us quite a good picture of the dinosaur. Muttaburrasaurus was an iguanodontid, related to Iguanodon. It lived in swampy places like the other iguanodontids. After the Australian find, experts have a better idea of how these creatures were distributed. Most of the other skeletons found have shown that the animals flourished in the Northern Hemisphere.

The head of Muttaburrasaurus is low and broad. A bony growth was found above the snout, but no one knows why it was there. Although much research has still to be done, the arrangement of the teeth shows that the creature was a plant-eater.

Weight not known
Length 20 feet (6 meters)
Found Queensland, Australia
Lived Late Cretaceous

Muttaburrasaurus

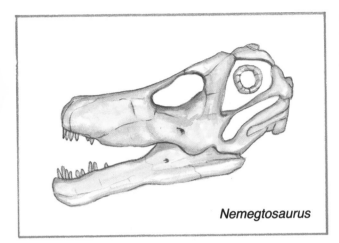

Nemegtosaurus

Nemegtosaurus

Nemegtosaurus was a diplodocid. Its most famous relative is Diplodocus, from which the family gets its name. Nemegtosaurus belonged to the large group of dinosaurs called sauropods, or "lizard feet." Although only a skull has been found, scientists have been able to show that Nemegtosaurus was similar to Diplodocus.

Nemegtosaurus was a large creature but it had very weak teeth, suitable only for eating plants. Nemegtosaurus and the other diplodocids were some of the longest plant-eaters ever to roam the Earth.

As more information about dinosaurs is collected, new theories are constantly being put forward. The idea that these creatures spent most of their lives in the water of swamps feeding on plants may no longer be true. Instead they probably ate low-growing plants on land, taking a great deal of food to satisfy their large bodies. These massive animals would have spent much of their time feeding. The peglike teeth would have bitten off pieces of plants which the animals probably swallowed whole.

Nemegtosaurus is the "lizard from Nemegt," a valley in Mongolia. If more remains are found and it is confirmed that the creature is a diplodocid, Nemegtosaurus will have been one of the last to live on the Earth.

Weight not known
Length 23 feet (7 meters)
Found Mongolia
Lived Late Cretaceous

Nodosaurus

Nodosaurus was a member of the ankylosaurs, or "fused lizards." This particular animal gives its name to a smaller group of dinosaurs called the nodosaurids, or "node lizards." The name comes from a strange arrangement of the bones, which were fused together to form large, shield-like plates. These plates covered most parts of the body, including the head. This distinctive armor plating consisted of a number of broad bands made up of alternating pieces of large and small rounded nodules.

From studies of other ankylosaurs it is known that the plates of armor had a number of tall spines, but so far these have not been recovered for Nodosaurus.

Nodosaurus

The skeleton of Nodosaurus found in the United States had no skull, and illustrations for this part of the body are based on other closely related ankylosaurs.

These creatures had small, weak teeth and probably fed on soft plant material which was growing close to the ground.

Weight not known
Length 18 feet (5.5 meters)
Found Wyoming and Kansas, USA
Lived Late Cretaceous

Opisthocoelicaudia

Opisthocoelicaudia

Studies of Opisthocoelicaudia are based on a single skeleton discovered in Mongolia's Gobi Desert. This dinosaur is a sauropod and would have had similar body proportions to Camarasaurus. Its thick legs supported a heavy body, and the creature probably walked with its tail straight out.

Although the skull of the skeleton was missing, the head of the creature has been reconstructed using heads from other camarasaurids.

Marks which were found on the bones of the skeleton could have been made by the teeth of meat-eating dinosaurs.

Weight not known
Length 40 feet (12 meters)
Found Gobi Desert, Mongolia
Lived Late Cretaceous

Ornitholestes

Ornitholestes was a coelurosaur. It is known as the "bird robber," because it caught and killed birds as well as other animals such as lizards and small mammals. These creatures were found in rocks of the same era as the dinosaur.

With powerful jaws and sharp teeth, Ornitholestes would have been capable of killing other animals.

Weight not known
Length 6 feet 6 inches (2 meters)
Found Wyoming, USA
Lived Late Jurassic

Ornitholestes

Ornithomimus

Ornithomimus, known as the "bird mimic," was a member of the ornithomimids, or "ostrich dinosaurs." A few remains of ornithomimids were found in 1869, but a reconstruction of the skeleton was possible only when more bones were unearthed in later years.

A study of the dinosaur showed that the tail was half the length of the body. Although Ornithomimus had long powerful fingers with which to collect its food, it did not have any teeth. However, it probably had a horny beak which would have broken up the food and made it easier to swallow.

Weight not known
Length 10 – 13 feet (3 – 4 meters)
Found western North America
Lived Late Cretaceous

Othnielia

Othnielia was similar in appearance to Hypsilophodon.

Like the other hypsilophodontids, it had long legs which enabled it to move quickly. Unfortunately, the skull of Othnielia has not been found, and so it is impossible to know how different it was from that of Hypsilophodon.

Othnielia was named after the American fossil collector Othniel Marsh, who had found many dinosaur remains in the late 1800s.

Weight not known
Length 4 feet 6 inches (1.4 meters)
Found North America
Lived Late Jurassic

Ornithomimus

Othnielia

O

Ouranosaurus

Ouranosaurus, or "brave monitor lizard," was a member of the iguanodontids. Remains of this dinosaur were first discovered in 1965 in West Africa.

Although it is related to the better-known Iguanodon, it has many unique features. It has been found only in Africa while other relatives, like Iguanodon, have been found in Europe, and Muttaburrasaurus has been unearthed in Australia.

Along the back of the dinosaur was a sail. The sail was held upright on a number of spines which came from the backbone. Other dinosaurs, like Spinosaurus, had similar sails. Blood may have passed through this sail, and it may have been used to control Ouranosaurus's body temperature. When it got too hot, heat passed out through the sail. When the creature became too cold, the large sail would have absorbed some of the heat from the sun – a kind of prehistoric solar panel!

The number of iguanodontids appeared to decrease when the hadrosaurids arrived. Iguanodontids could compete with hypsilophodontids because they had different needs, but they could not compete with the hadrosaurids, which may have needed the same kind of food.

Weight not known
Length 23 feet (7 meters)
Found Niger, West Africa
Lived Early Cretaceous

Oviraptor

Oviraptor belonged to a family of dinosaurs known as "egg thieves." These are small creatures, the first of which was discovered in the Mongolian Desert in 1923. Oviraptor was found buried on top of a nest of Protoceratops eggs. This is why it was given the name "egg thief."

An examination of the head showed that Oviraptor had powerful jaws which opened and closed the beak. The bottom jaw arched upward, enabling the creature to exert a great deal of pressure on anything which it grasped. This jaw was probably capable of crushing bones as well as eggs.

The bones of the hands were arranged so that Oviraptor could grasp things fairly easily. Each finger had a claw, and the largest was on the first digit.

Studies of several Oviraptor skulls show that there may have been a number of different species. Some heads had crests. Two skulls discovered in Mongolia are still being studied, but early research shows that they are smooth with large eye sockets. It is possible that these skulls belonged to young animals.

Weight not known
Length 6 feet (1.8 meters)
Found southern Mongolia
Lived Late Cretaceous

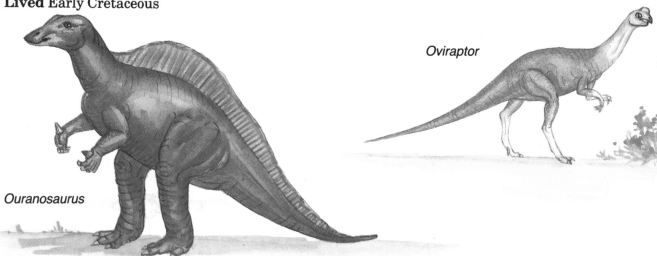

Ouranosaurus

Oviraptor

Pachycephalosaurus

Pachycephalosaurus gives its name to the group known as pachycephalosaurs, or "thick-headed lizards." The first find, in the bed of the Judith River, in Montana, was a tooth. Further discoveries have been made, but no complete skeleton has been found yet. Scientists studying Pachycephalosaurus think that it was probably about 26 feet (8 meters) in length.

As so few bones have been discovered, experts have tried to build up a body framework based on guesswork and information compiled from other animals in the same family.

We know that these dinosaurs had thick skulls, most of which were decorated with a series of spines and knobs. The animals may have used these in combat, in much the same way as deer use their antlers today. The especially thick skull of Pachycephalosaurus gave the creature's head a domed appearance. Some of these skull bones were more than 10 inches (25 centimeters) thick. Pachycephalosaurus was the largest of these bonehead dinosaurs and had the biggest, thickest, and most decorated skull.

It has been suggested that these creatures roamed in herds with a male in charge of the group.

Weight not known
Length 15 – 26 feet (4.6 – 8 meters)
Found western North America
Lived Late Cretaceous

Parasaurolophus

Parasaurolophus was a hadrosaurid. The distinctive feature of this group is the great variation in crests found on the heads.

From remains recovered, scientists have found that Parasaurolophus had the most distinctive and showy crests of any of the hadrosaurids. Growing over the top of the head was a long tube, or "horn," which measured about 39 inches (1 meter) in length.

It was thought that this horn could have acted as a snorkel when the animal was in water. This idea has been rejected because there is no opening at the end of the tube.

The nostrils were positioned normally at the front of the animal's snout, from which tubes ran up into the horn and then down again into the mouth. Each horn had two tubes going up and two coming down. The tubes may have been used by the dinosaurs for making noises, either for attracting their own kind or for warning of impending danger.

The large crests also puzzled the experts. The most likely explanation is that they served as signals, telling other animals that they belonged to the same group.

Weight not known
Length 33 feet (10 meters)
Found New Mexico and Utah, USA;
  Alberta, Canada
Lived Late Cretaceous

Pachycephalosaurus

Parasaurolophus

P

Parksosaurus

Parksosaurus was another of the hypsilophodontids and one of the last of this group of dinosaurs to be found on the Earth. Remains of hypsilophodontids have told us a lot about many of these creatures, but only an incomplete skull of Parksosaurus has been discovered so far.

Parksosaurus means "Parks's lizard." It takes its name from a Canadian paleontologist. A study of the skull showed that Parksosaurus, with its unique arrangement of the teeth, was different from other hypsilophodontids.

When Parksosaurus died it fell on its left side and was covered with sand. As a result most of

Pentaceratops

Parksosaurus

the upper part of the skeleton, including part of the skull, was lost. Perhaps it was attacked by other creatures once it had died, or it might have disintegrated because it was not completely covered.

Although Parksosaurus was one of the last hypsilophodontids to live on the Earth, it is one of the least known because of the incomplete nature of the finds.

Weight 143 – 154 pounds (65 – 70 kilograms)
Length estimate 8 feet (2.4 meters)
Found Alberta, Canada
Lived Late Cretaceous

Pentaceratops

Pentaceratops, the "five-horned face," was a member of the group known as long-frilled ceratopsids.

The variety of horns on the head made this particular ceratopsid unique. It had more of these outgrowths than any other horned dinosaur. Two of the largest horns were on the brow, with two smaller horns on the sides of the face. These were really outgrowths of bone. The final horn, which was small, was on the end of the snout.

When horned hadrosaurids were first discovered, various suggestions were put forward as to the purpose of these outgrowths. Latest theories are that, as with modern deer, the horns helped to create some form of social order. In deer and antelopes the horns are also used as a means of establishing territorial claims.

The ceratopsian frills have also been the subject of much discussion. It seems possible that these frills were also connected with the dinosaur's behavior. Creatures with long frills would have been able to use them for display purposes. This was more likely than using them to ward off enemies.

Weight not known
Length estimate 20 feet (6 meters)
Found New Mexico, USA
Lived Late Cretaceous

Plateosaurus

Plateosaurus is known as the "flat lizard." It was a member of the prosauropods, a large group of dinosaurs found over much of the world. Their remains have been unearthed in every continent except Antarctica. Plateosaurus is the best known and probably the most common of these early dinosaurs because of the large amount of material discovered in more than fifty different places in Europe.

Plateosaurus

Plateosaurus had a long neck and was able to stand on its back legs, so it could easily collect plant material from trees. It would also have taken plants from the ground.

Its head was small and at the end of a long neck made up of smaller bones, so it was able to move easily. Extremely heavy, well-developed limb bones supported the large body. The hind legs, which carried most of the weight, were stronger than the front ones.

Two of the five fingers on the hand were less developed than the others. One had a scythe-like claw. This may have been used by the dinosaur to collect food, or to defend itself from its enemies.

Weight not known
Length 26 feet (8 meters)
Found Germany, France, England, Switzerland
Lived Late Triassic

P

Procompsognathus

Procompsognathus means "before Compsognathus," which in turn means "pretty jaw."

Procompsognathus was a small coelurosaur. It was one of the earliest dinosaurs to appear on the Earth. Like its relatives it was lightly built, with powerful hind limbs for speedy movement. Coelurosaurs are divided into a number of groups. Procompsognathus belonged to the group of coelophysids, or "hollow forms." These creatures had hollow bones in their bodies.

Procompsognathus could balance well when running by holding its tail straight out behind. The tail probably also acted as a support when the dinosaur stopped.

The teeth of the animal seem to show that it was a meat-eater and, because it could run fast, it was able to chase, capture, and kill small lizardlike creatures. Procompsognathus may also have removed flesh from dead animals. It would have used its clawed hands to catch food and put it in its mouth.

The creature had a small head, about 3 inches (8 centimeters) in length, but it was armed with powerful pointed and curved teeth for eating its food.

Weight not known
Length 4 feet (1.2 meters)
Found southwest Germany
Lived Late Triassic

Protoceratops

Protoceratops is one of the earliest forms of horned dinosaurs yet found. It was probably the ancestor of many other creatures.

Protoceratops, or the "first horned face," had an extremely large head with a bony frill. This stretched from the skull and had very powerful jaw muscles attached to it. This horny frill may also have protected the dinosaur's neck and shoulders.

Protoceratops' nests, which were discovered in the Mongolian Desert, showed how the dinosaurs had laid their eggs. Females made holes in the sand and then laid their eggs in a circle. The eggs were then covered with sand so that they would be kept warm and eventually hatch. We do not know whether Protoceratops took any further interest in the eggs after they had been laid.

A study of the eggs showed that many had baby dinosaurs developing inside them. This gave scientists an insight into this part of the dinosaur's cycle. The discovery of several nests grouped together persuaded scientists to revise their theories on the behavior of these prehistoric reptiles. Until then, only birds had been associated with nesting in colonies.

Weight 1.5 US tons (1.4 tonnes)
Length 5 feet 10 inches (1.8 meters)
Found Mongolia
Lived Late Cretaceous

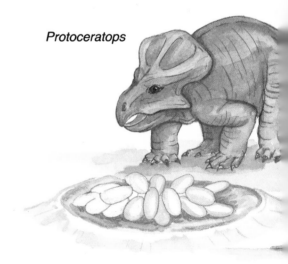
Protoceratops

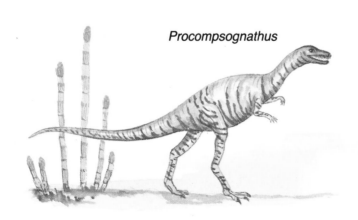
Procompsognathus

Psittacosaurus

Psittacosaurus is known as the "parrot lizard." It was a ceratopsian, or "horned-faced" dinosaur. These animals lived during the latter stages of the Age of Reptitles, appearing on the Earth during the early part of the Cretaceous period.

Psittacosaurs were strange creatures with horns on each side of the face and a snout which ended in a parrotlike beak. They used their beak to chop off pieces of plant material on which they fed.

Scientists now believe that Psittacosaurus represents a stage between two groups of dinosaurs. The creature had some of the same characteristics as the ornithopods and also the curved, parrotlike beak of the ceratopsians, which is formed by a separate bone.

Young Psittacosaurus skulls which were found in Mongolia were between 1.1 and 1.6 inches (28 and 42 millimeters) in length.

Weight 50 pounds (22.7 kilograms)
Length 2 feet 7 inches – 6 feet (80 – 150 centimeters)
Found Mongolia, southern Siberia, east and northeast China
Lived Early Cretaceous

Rhoetosaurus

Few dinosaur remains have been discovered on the Australian continent, so any find causes great excitement among scientists. This was true of Rhoetosaurus, which is a cetiosaurid, or "whale lizard." The group gets its name from a number of bones discovered in England toward the end of the nineteenth century. Without studying the bones carefully, the collectors suggested that they were from aquatic creatures. Later research has shown that this was not so.

These cetiosaurids were the first of the sauropods, or "lizard feet." Even though they were some of the first sauropods to evolve, they were large creatures. Remains from many parts of the world show that the cetiosaurs were widely distributed, although Rhoetosaurus was confined to Australia.

Rhoetosaurus is known as the "Rhoetos lizard." Rhoetos is a giant in Greek mythology. No complete skeleton has been found yet, but discoveries in the 1920s revealed first a tail, then bones from the dinosaur's hip region.

It has not been possible to build up a skeleton from the small amount of material recovered. However, experts measured the thighbone, which was 5 feet (1.5 meters) long, and from this figure they have been able to estimate the length of Rhoetosaurus.

Weight not known
Length 39 feet (12 meters)
Found western Australia
Lived Middle Jurassic

Psittacosaurus

Rhoetosaurus

Saltopus

Saltopus or "leaping foot," was a small coelurosaur which was discovered in a sandstone quarry in northern Scotland in the British Isles. Like the other coelurosaurs, Saltopus was lightly built and able to move quickly. After studying the long back legs, scientists think that the creature was able to jump and leap.

Because the creature was so fast and agile, it is possible that it fed on insects and small lizardlike animals which roamed Scotland at this time.

On the front limb of each hand there were five fingers. The first three were larger than the other two.

Weight 2 pounds (900 grams)
Length 2 feet (60 centimeters)
Found northern Scotland
Lived Late Triassic

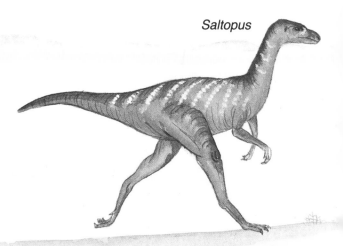
Saltopus

Saurolophus

Saurolophus, the "ridged lizard," was one of the hadrosaurid "duckbill" dinosaurs. Like the other hadrosaurids it had a crest which consisted of a distinctive bony ridge running along the skull. This ended in a small spike. Several different species of this dinosaur have been found, each with its own peculiar ridge. Comparison has shown that there is considerable variation in the size and shape of the spike at the back of the ridge.

Remains of Saurolophus have been widely discovered in Asia and on the North American continent. It is interesting that the spike found on the Asian species is much larger than that on the American species.

The duckbill was used to chop off plant material for food.

Weight not known
Length 33 feet (10 meters)
Found North America, East Asia
Lived Late Cretaceous

Saurornithoides

Saurornithoides has given its name to a group of dinosaurs known as the saurornithoidids. Two incomplete skeletons of these animals were found close to each other in the Gobi Desert. In one discovery the legs, feet, pelvis, and backbone were unearthed and in the other a large part of the skull.

The creature was named "birdlike lizard from Mongolia." A study of the feet of Saurornithoides showed a second toe which was shorter than the others and could be held above the ground when the creature walked. This toe had

48

Saurolophus

Saurornithoides

a sharp claw which the dinosaur probably used to defend itself.

The dinosaur had a large brain, so it could co-ordinate the movements of its extremely well-developed body and move very quickly. It also had large eyes, so it was probably out and about at night preying on other animals, including small mammals.

Weight not known
Length 6 feet 6 inches (2 meters)
Found Mongolia
Lived Late Cretaceous

Scelidosaurus

Scelidosaurus, the "limb lizard," was first discovered in England by the famous nineteenth-century fossil collector Richard Owen. The original bones, which he claimed all came from the same creature, have since been identified as belonging to other dinosaurs as well. This creature was an early armored dinosaur.

One feature of the skeleton was that the rear thighbones were longer than the front ones. Scelidosaurus moved slowly and would have been open to attack from meat-eating creatures if it had not been covered with armor plating.

Scelidosaurus

There were large numbers of cone-shaped, bony studs arranged in rows along the back. They were extremely hard and would have damaged the teeth of the strongest predator.

There is an interesting arrangement of these projections just behind the head, where they form groups of three. The reason for this particular grouping is not clear. It is possibly an added form of protection, but it does not occur anywhere else on the armor plating.

Scelidosaurus had extremely small rough-edged teeth with which it chewed its plant food.

Weight not known
Length 13 feet (4 meters)
Found southern England
Lived Early Jurassic

Segnosaurus

Segnosaurus belonged to a group of dinosaurs named after it, the segnosaurids. Scientists have found the members of the group to be different from other flesh-eating dinosaurs, so they have put them in a different family.

Segnosaurus is the "slow lizard." Bones have been found belonging to three animals which make up the group of segnosaurids. They are Erlikosaurus, Segnosaurus, and Nanshiungosaurus.

Close examination of the finds showed that this group had some puzzling features. At the end of the face was a toothless beak. There were no teeth in the front of the jaw, but those at the back were bladelike and capable of slicing leaves. The hips were birdlike and very different from those of the other carnosaurs, which were lizardlike.

No one is certain how Segnosaurus lived, but some scientists seem to think that it fed on plants, because its teeth are very different from those of other flesh-eating dinosaurs.

Weight not known
Length 30 feet (9 meters)
Found southern Mongolia
Lived Late Cretaceous

Segnosaurus

Shantungosaurus

The "lizard from Shantung" was another of the hadrosaurine duckbills. It was the largest member of this group of dinosaurs. Its relatives include better-known species like Anatosaurus and Edmontosaurus.

The best remains of this creature consist of an almost complete skeleton which was found in China.

Although its basic body type was similar to the Canadian Edmontosaurus, Shantungosaurus was larger than its North American relative. A man standing beside Shantungosaurus would have reached only to the dinosaur's knee!

As in other duckbills the front of the dinosaur's mouth had no teeth, but the powerful jaws enabled it to chew its food satisfactorily. It is also likely that the dinosaur would have collected more food than it could deal with at one time. It would store the food in its cheeks, continuing to chew it before swallowing. Without any body protection, animals like Shantungosaurus might have made for the nearest dense thicket to avoid the attention of meat-eating carnosaurs. Some scientists think that it might even have taken to the water to avoid predators.

Weight not known
Length 39 – 49 feet (12 – 15 meters)
Found Shantung, China
Lived Late Cretaceous

Shantungosaurus

Silvisaurus

Silvisaurus, the "forest lizard," was discovered in the United States. It was a nodosaurid ankylosaur. Although no complete skeleton has been found, enough of the remains were found for scientists to reconstruct the creature.

The dinosaur was heavily armored like its relatives and had a variety of plates on its back. Some might have been round, and others many-sided. These were thick enough to protect the animal from its enemies. The shoulders were protected by sharp spines.

As in many other ankylosaurs, a number of

Silvisaurus

plates protruded from the tail of Silvisaurus. However, it seems that the dinosaur lacked the club at the end of the tail (see Ankylosaurus). A sideways movement of the spiked tail would probably have caused serious injury to other dinosaurs.

The mouth of this nodosaurid was unusual. It had pointed teeth close to the front of the upper jaw. Most other dinosaurs in this group had a large horny beak. In Silvisaurus the upper part of the beak was probably smaller than in many of its dinosaur relatives.

Weight not known
Length 13 feet (4 meters)
Found Kansas, USA
Lived Early Cretaceous

Spinosaurus

Spinosaurus, whose name means "spiny lizard," was a carnosaur. This dinosaur and its relatives were extremely large flesh-eaters.

Experts are particularly interested in the

Spinosaurus

Staurikosaurus

spinosaurids because of the spines growing out from their backs. These spines were probably there to support a large skin sail, which may have controlled the body temperature. In cold conditions heat could be obtained from the sun, and in hot weather it could be lost to the atmosphere.

Spinosaurus was discovered in Africa. It may be that these sails developed as a means of controlling body temperature in a hot climate.

Weight 7 US tons (6.4 tonnes)
Length 40 feet (12 meters)
Found Egypt, Niger
Lived Late Cretaceous

Staurikosaurus

Staurikosaurus was an early dinosaur belonging to the group staurikosaurids, to which it gives its name. Staurikosaurids are "cross lizards," a name which comes from the Southern Cross star group. These dinosaurs walked on two legs. Staurikosaurus was one of the first members of this group.

It was an agile animal with long legs and could move very fast. The head was comparatively large for the size of the body, and inside the jaws were teeth sharp enough to cut up flesh.

Weight not known
Length 6 feet 6 inches (2 meters)
Found southern Brazil
Lived Late Middle Triassic

Stegosaurus

Stegosaurus

The most noticeable feature of the stegosaurids, or "plated lizards," is the arrangement of large plates and spines on the neck, back and tail. No one is certain how the plates were arranged, although they are generally shown upright.

The reason for the plates is unclear, but they may have been used to adjust the level of body heat. At first it was thought that they were for protection and were shown flat along the body. The creature supposedly used its vicious tail spikes to defend itself against enemies.

In spite of their size and fearsome appearance these dinosaurs had very small teeth. They fed on plants, probably by browsing on the ground or removing leaves from trees.

Weight 2 US tons (1.8 tonnes)
Length 30 feet (9 meters)
Found Colorado, Oklahoma, Utah, and
 Wyoming, USA
Lived Late Jurassic

Stenonychosaurus

Stenonychosaurus was the "narrow clawed lizard." Studies have shown that it had quite a large brain. The brain would have helped the creature to control its agile limbs and reflex actions, necessary in an animal that spent its

Stenonychosaurus

time in pursuit of food. Well-developed senses including large eyes and possibly good hearing would also have helped when hunting.

There are close similarities between this species and Saurornithoides.

Weight 60 – 100 pounds (27 – 45 kilograms)
Length 6 feet 6 inches (2 meters)
Found Alberta, Canada
Lived Late Cretaceous

Struthiosaurus

Struthiosaurus was another nodosaurid ankylosaur. It was the "ostrich lizard." Remains have come from various parts of Europe, but unfortunately an entire skeleton is not yet known. Struthiosaurus is the smallest of the nodosaurids so far discovered. It is known to be about half the length of some of its relatives like Acanthopholis and Nodosaurus.

A study of the armor plating on the body shows that it is of five different kinds. A number of sharp plates provided protection for the tail and hips, with a combination of smaller spikes

Struthiosaurus

and knobs covering other parts of the tail and the sides of the body. The vulnerable shoulder area was guarded by some large spines, and the neck by plates which had both a big spine and smaller bones.

Weight not known
Length 6 feet (1.8 meters)
Found Austria, Hungary, Romania, France
Lived Late Cretaceous

Styracosaurus

Styracosaurus, the "spiked lizard," was a short-frilled ceratopsid. Its short frill has intrigued experts since it was discovered. It was similar to the frills on many other ceratopsids, because it was surrounded by typical nodules of bone. However, these nodules increased in size toward the back of the frill.

This frill probably served two purposes. It would have warned other creatures to stay away, but it would also have been useful when Styracosaurus wanted to attract a mate. It may also have been used for defense.

Styracosaurus

This plant-eating dinosaur had a large dangerous-looking horn at the end of its snout. This would have been useful in protecting the creature against its enemies. A smaller horn above each of the eyes would also have been used in defense and as a protective feature.

All the species of short-frilled ceratopsians so far discovered have come from the North American continent.

Styracosaurus had strong jaws and was able to chew tough plants.

Weight not known
Length 18 feet (5.5 meters)
Found Alberta, Canada; Montana, USA
Lived Late Cretaceous

Syntarsus

Syntarsus was a coelurosaur, a "hollow-tailed lizard". Like the other members of the group, this creature had slender bones which made it agile and able to move fast. Syntarsus used its quick reactions and speed when giving chase to other animals which it needed to catch for food.

The long legs show the creature's adaptation for speed. A study of the bones shows that they were lightly built. Having to carry less weight was an important feature in any creature which had to get from one place to another as quickly as possible. The heavily built dinosaurs, like Stegosaurus, had to be protected from their enemies because they could not move quickly enough to escape. Syntarsus did not need any form of protection because it was fast enough to escape when other larger creatures threatened it.

The long arms were shorter than the hind legs but had hands with claws. These would have been useful for picking up food and directing it toward the mouth. They might also have been used by the creature for removing flesh from the carcasses of dead animals.

The creature would have moved about the land on its hind legs, feeding on lizards, small dinosaurs, and possibly insects and eggs.

Syntarsus was given the name "fused tarsus" because of bones in the ankle which were found to be joined, or fused, together.

When remains of dinosaurs such as Syntarsus are found the outer skin covering is usually absent, having decayed much more quickly than the harder bones. When reconstructing these creatures, scientists have to rely on guesswork, but their guesses are based on careful study.

In some illustrations of Syntarsus the dinosaur is shown with a plume decorating the back of the head, and a body covered with feathery scales. Few people now believe that this was the way Syntarsus looked.

The remains of Syntarsus were discovered in Zimbabwe. Although found together, the bones belonged to many skeletons, none of which was complete. Syntarsus belonged to the group of dinosaurs known as the coelophysids, named after Coelophysis. A comparison of Syntarsus with Coelophysis has shown many similarities between them. However, many differences have also been revealed. For example, the skull of Syntarsis is shorter than that of Coelophysis.

Weight 66 pounds (30 kilograms)
Length 9 feet 9 inches (3 meters)
Found Zimbabwe
Lived Late Triassic

Syntarsus

T

Tarbosaurus

Tarbosaurus was a tyrannosaurid. The best-known member of this group is Tyrannosaurus. Because of its lighter bones Tarbosaurus was not as heavy as Tyrannosaurus. Yet studies of its remains show that some individuals grew to a larger size. Estimates suggest that it was between 33 and 46 feet (10 and 14 meters) in length.

Many skeletons of the large, meat-eating Tarbosaurus have been found, but the creature has not yet been fully described. The results of preliminary work have been published and show that the dinosaur was a lot like Tyrannosaurus.

A study of the creature's upper jaw proved interesting. It showed that there were more than twenty extremely large, knife-shaped teeth which would have dealt efficiently with the flesh on which the animal fed.

Standing on its hind legs Tarbosaurus measured between 14 feet 6 inches and 20 feet (4.5 and 6 meters) in height.

Weight not known
Length 33 – 46 feet (10 – 14 meters)
Found Mongolia
Lived Late Cretaceous

Thecodontosaurus

Thecodontosaurus

Thecodontosaurus, the "socket-toothed lizard," was a prosauropod and related to Plateosaurus. It was a member of the group known as anchisaurids, all of which were small and rather lightly built. The first clue to this particular animal came when a piece of the jawbone was discovered in southern England in 1843.

Studies of the skeleton show that the hind limbs were stronger than the front limbs. The hind limbs had thumbs with extremely large claws and were probably used when the animal went hunting.

Because only a few remains have been found, experts have suggested that they might even belong to the young of the plateosaurids. This could be confirmed only if more material were found.

Thecodontosaurus may have moved in two ways—upright on its hind legs and on all fours.

Living in dry upland areas, the creature appears to have gone foraging for food.

Weight not known
Length 7 feet (2 meters)
Found southern England, possibly South Africa, possibly Australia
Lived Late Triassic and Early Jurassic

Tarbosaurus

Thescelosaurus

Thescelosaurus

Thescelosaurus is the "beautiful lizard." It is known from a number of fragments as well as a complete skeleton. The dinosaur has been placed in a group of its own, the thescelosaurids, which belonged to the hypsilophodontids.

Although these animals were much smaller than the iguanodontids, their leg bones seem to be very similar. Like the other hypsilophodontids, Thescelosaurus was built for agility and speed.

There are many similarities between the teeth of Thescelosaurus and Hypsilophodon, although the ridges on the teeth of Thescelosaurus are very different from those on the teeth of Hypsilophodon. One of the similarities is that there were no teeth in the front part of the top jaw.

Small bony plates may have been present in rows along the middle of the creature's back.

Weight not known
Length 11 feet (3.4 meters)
Found Alberta and Saskatchewan, Canada; Montana and Wyoming, USA
Lived at the end of the Late Cretaceous

Titanosaurus

Titanosaurus gave its name to a group of dinosaurs known as the titanosaurids. The name means "titanic lizard," referring to the Titans, giants of Greek mythology. It is therefore quite misleading, because this sauropod was much smaller than many of the other dinosaurs in its group.

Titanosaurus has been found in many places, and remains have been collected in countries as far apart as Argentina, Hungary, and India. In earlier times, with a larger land mass, it was possible for animals to move about much more freely. The back of Titanosaurus may have been covered with small, armored, shieldlike plates. The long whiplash tail tapered toward the end and might have been used for attacking enemies. At least some members of this group of dinosaurs had armor, which sets them apart from other sauropod groups.

Weight not known
Length 40 feet (12 meters)
Found Europe, India, Indochina, South America
Lived Late Cretaceous

Titanosaurus

Triceratops

Torosaurus

Torosaurus

Torosaurus was a long-frilled ceratopsid and had the honor of being the largest animal in the group. It also had the longest frill of any horned dinosaur so far discovered. Its name means "bull lizard" because of the massive size of the skull, which measured more than 8 feet (2.5 meters) from front to back. This makes it the largest skull of any land-living animal found so far.

There were large horns above the eyes and a smaller one on the nose.

Weight 8 – 9 US tons (7.3 – 8.2 tonnes)
Length 25 feet (7.6 meters)
Found Montana and Texas, USA
Lived Late Cretaceous

Triceratops

Triceratops was a short-frilled ceratopsid. The name means "three-horned face," and refers to the three extremely large and menacing horns on the face.

Many skulls of Triceratops have been uncovered and scientists have been able to identify no fewer than fifteen different species of the creature.

There are still disagreements about the animal's appearance, which varies from one illustration to another. The horns of Triceratops are its most distinctive feature. One grew out from the nose, and the other two were situated one above each eye. Like the other short-frilled ceratopsids, Triceratops had a characteristic, moderate-sized frill. Along the back edge of this frill were a number of lumps of bone.

Weight 9.4 US tons (8.5 tonnes)
Length 30 feet (9 meters)
Found USA, western Canada
Lived Late Cretaceous

Tyrannosaurus

Tyrannosaurus, the "tyrant lizard," is probably the best known of all the dinosaurs. Experts once believed that it was one of the most ferocious creatures ever to roam the Earth. They believed that Tyrannosaurus always caught other animals for its food. But today scientists think that Tyrannosaurus was also a scavenger, picking up material left by other animals or eating animals that had died from disease or other causes. Some experts believe that an animal as huge as Tyrannosaurus would have had great difficulty in moving fast enough to capture and kill other animals.

Tyrannosaurus was a carnosaur, and had serrated teeth rather like the teeth of a saw. They measured as long as 7.25 inches (18.5 centimeters) in length, and would have been capable of tearing apart flesh. The teeth were arranged inside a jaw measuring 4 feet 10 inches (1.5 meters) in length. Compared to the large hind legs, the front arms were very small, but they were extremely strong.

Weight 7 US tons (6.4 tonnes)
Length 39 feet (12 meters)
Found Alberta, Canada; Montana, USA
Lived Late Cretaceous

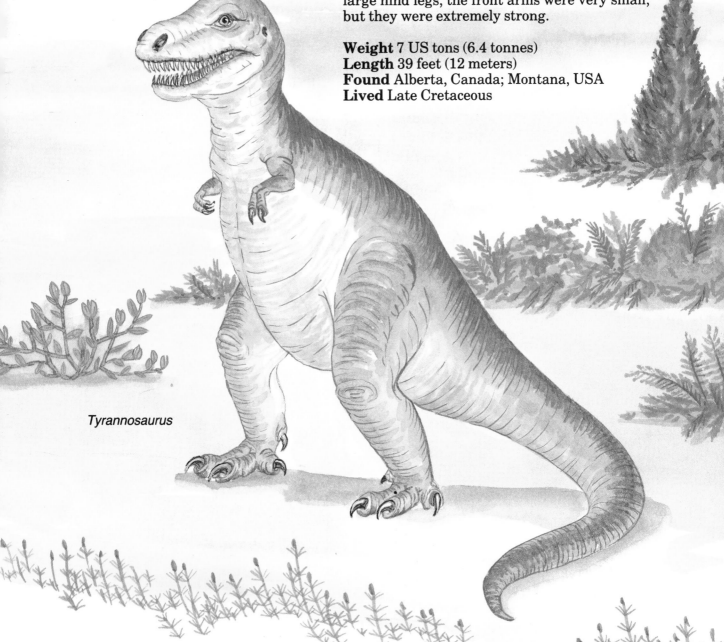

Tyrannosaurus

U

"Ultrasaurus"

It takes a long time to study dinosaur finds once they are discovered. "Ultrasaurus," which was first discovered in 1979, has yet to be given a proper scientific name because studies are not complete.

However, from the first investigations it seems that this creature may have been even bigger than Brachiosaurus. Initial research suggests that it may have been up to 100 feet (30.5 meters) long. This would make it the largest dinosaur ever discovered.

With modern "search" techniques it is now possible to find more and more bones of new dinosaurs, and to learn new facts about them as footprints and other discoveries are made.

Weight estimate 150 US tons (136 tonnes)
Length estimate 100 feet (30.5 meters)
Found Colorado, USA
Lived Late Jurassic

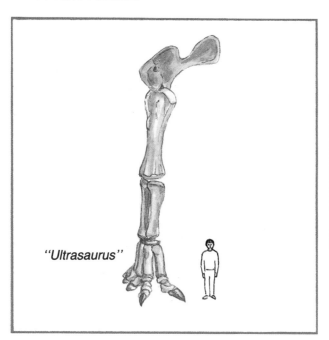

"Ultrasaurus"

Velociraptor

Velociraptor means the "swift plunderer." The creature was a coelurosaur and belonged to the group known as dromaeosaurids—the "running lizards." Until some work was published in 1969 most people had thought of dinosaurs as rather lethargic creatures. Research showed that dinosaurs like Velociraptor were capable of moving fast. Further studies have shown that these creatures were some of the fastest animals to inhabit the Earth. This, and their fierce nature, made them extremely successful dinosaurs. Since the discovery of the first dromaeosaurids, further remains have been found and research into their significance continues.

Velociraptor had a lower and narrower head than other dromaeosaurids. No one knows why this is so, although some experts suggest it might have had something to do with the creature's lifestyle and particularly with the food which it caught and ate.

An interesting discovery was made in 1971 when a specimen of Velociraptor was found. It was still attached to a Protoceratops which it may have captured. Both creatures had died, with Velociraptor still clinging to the head of Protoceratops.

Weight not known
Length 6 feet (1.8 meters)
Found Mongolia; Kazakhstan, USSR; China
Lived Late Cretaceous

Velociraptor

Yaverlandia

Yaverlandia has been named after Yaverland, a place on the Isle of Wight, off the south coast of England, where the discovery was made. This creature belonged to the pachycephalosaurids, the "bonehead dinosaurs."

The remains of Yaverlandia show that it was the oldest of the boneheads and arrived on the scene before any of the others so far discovered. A distinctive feature was the thickened area of bone which was found on the top of the skull. No one is quite sure why this toughened bone was there. It has been suggested that the males may have engaged in combat by butting each other with the tops of their thickened skulls, rather like today's deer.

Studies of the head and backbones of the boneheads have shown that these parts absorbed the impact of blows during a fight, preventing injury to the dinosaur. The females of the boneheads appear to have thick skulls like the males, but probably did not take part in these encounters.

The creatures had long tails which were used for supporting the rest of the body when at rest. These dinosaurs were not able to move quickly, and fed on plants.

Weight not known
Length 3 feet (90 centimeters)
Found Isle of Wight
Lived Early Cretaceous

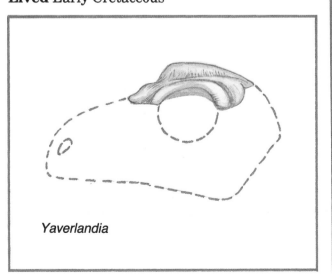

Yaverlandia

Zephyrosaurus

Zephyrosaurus, the "west wind lizard," was another of the hypsilophodontids, related to the better-known Hypsilophodon. So far, only partial remains have been found in the United States. These remains include the skull and some of the vertebrae, bones which make up the backbone.

Although there were many similarities between this species and Hypsilophodon, there was a small bony projection on each side of the cheek in Zephyrosaurus. Inside the jaw the teeth showed a similar pattern to those of most other hypsilophodontids. They had ridges, well-designed for chopping up the plant food which formed the bulk of the diet of Zephyrosaurus. The family name of "high ridge tooth" refers to these teeth.

Animals which can run fast are often meat-eaters. In the case of Zephyrosaurus speed was probably a useful means of escaping from enemies. If these dinosaurs had not been able to move quickly, they would soon have become easy prey for the larger flesh-eating creatures which shared their world.

Weight not known
Length 6 feet (1.8 meters)
Found Montana, USA
Lived Early Cretaceous

Zephyrosaurus

Dinosaur History

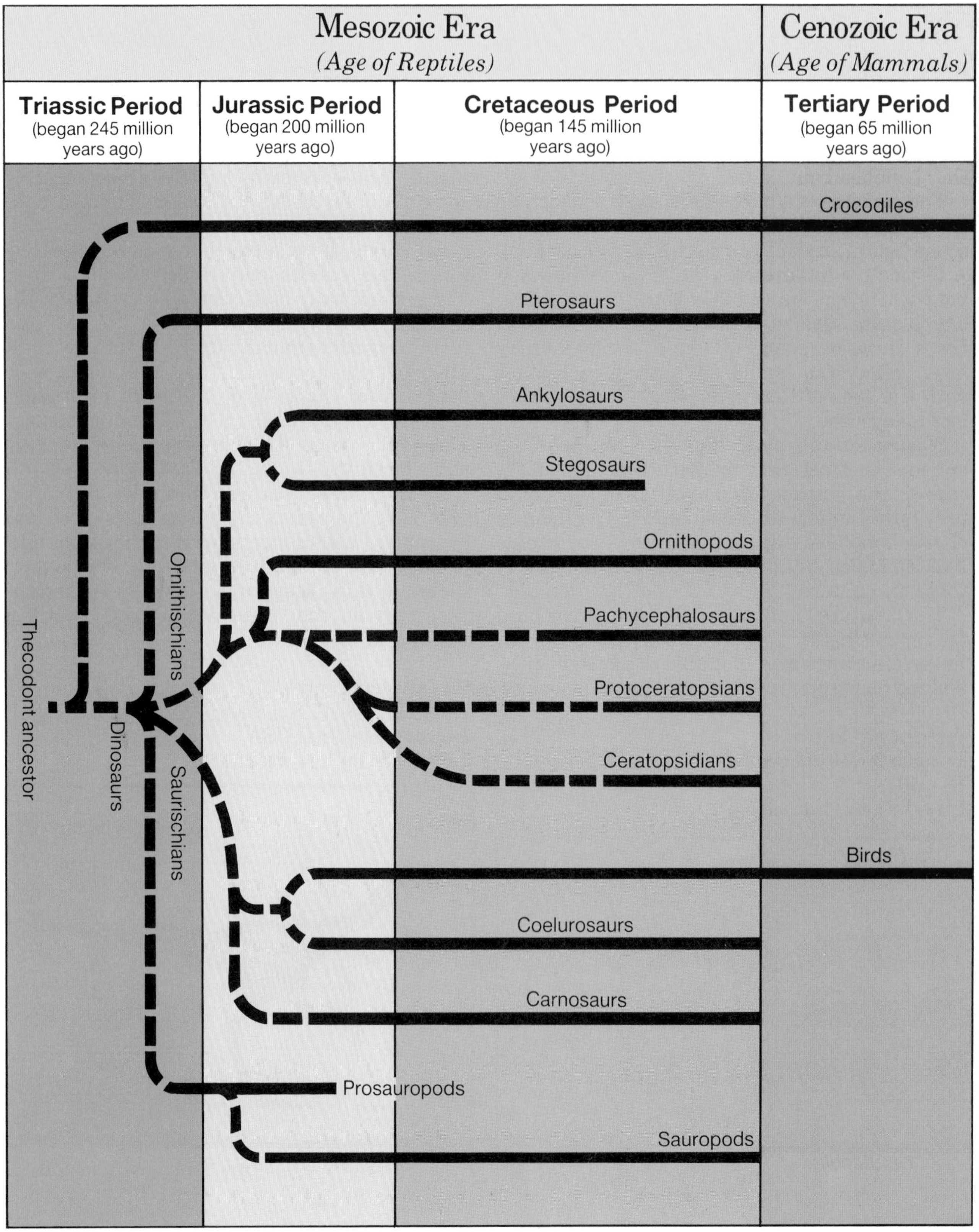

Mesozoic Era (Age of Reptiles)			Cenozoic Era (Age of Mammals)
Triassic Period (began 245 million years ago)	**Jurassic Period** (began 200 million years ago)	**Cretaceous Period** (began 145 million years ago)	**Tertiary Period** (began 65 million years ago)

Crocodiles

Pterosaurs

Ankylosaurs

Stegosaurs

Ornithopods

Pachycephalosaurs

Protoceratopsians

Ceratopsidians

Birds

Coelurosaurs

Carnosaurs

Prosauropods

Sauropods

Thecodont ancestor

Ornithischians

Dinosaurs

Saurischians